Some Wars
Never End

To Jeanie, Robert,
Jacob and Miriam

Enjoy!

Shirley Ann Newman

Some Wars Never End

Memoirs of a Jewish Resistance Fighter in Nazi-Occupied France

---

by Shirley Ann Newman

BITTERSWEET PUBLISHING CO.
P.O. BOX 30407
BAKERSFIELD, CA 93385

Table Of Contents

Dedication

During the era of the Third Reich of Germany, whose poison permeated other nations, infecting, contaminating, or just "paralyzing" their populations, there were millions of resisters.

All of them did not feel courageous: most were probable terrified, yet did not see themselves as having any justifiable option but to commit themselves to opposing the evils—the unspeakable, the almost unimaginable cruelty—of Nazism and the purveyors and supporters of that doctrine.

The risks were unmistakable. Not only did resisters put their personal lives in jeopardy/ there was always the possibility of repercussions to their families, neighbors, to whole communities. Innumerable deaths were meted out to many—many completely uninvolved—as retribution for the deeds of those who opposed the racism and anti-Semitism sweeping through Europe like uncontrollable wildfire.

Resisters belonged to underground movements, or, although not actually "sworn members," cooperated with these organized groups. Gentile individuals helped Jewish friends, colleagues, employers, or employees to hide or to escape. They provided shelter, food, and other resources. A wealth of documentation, including personal accounts of survivors attest to their courage in behaving ethically and loyally. They lived up to what is most admirable in human society as well as in the religious value articulated by the command not to stand idly by while your neighbor bleeds.

Among these righteous are the most righteous to whom I dedicate this book. It is specifically to the Christian pastors in France, who used church buildings and various other structures as "safe houses" to hide those in danger, and served as links in the chain of resisters who smuggled out of the country thousands of the victims of the German occupiers and of the collaborating Vichy government of France. Without having personally known Max Neuman and most of the others in flight—except as Jewish persons vulnerable to arrest, torture and execution—pastors, committed to the true teachings of their faith, chose not to stand idly by. Max Neuman, who defied the law requiring him to register as a Jew, joined the maquis, the French underground movement. After eighteen months as a freedom fighter, he took the equally perilous initiative to attempt his escape from France. Without help from these pastors and others, he faced almost certain capture and death.

I can conceive of no higher level of human nobility than the acts of his anonymous benefactors.

—Shirley Ann Newman

Max the Parisian (a favorite portrait of his)

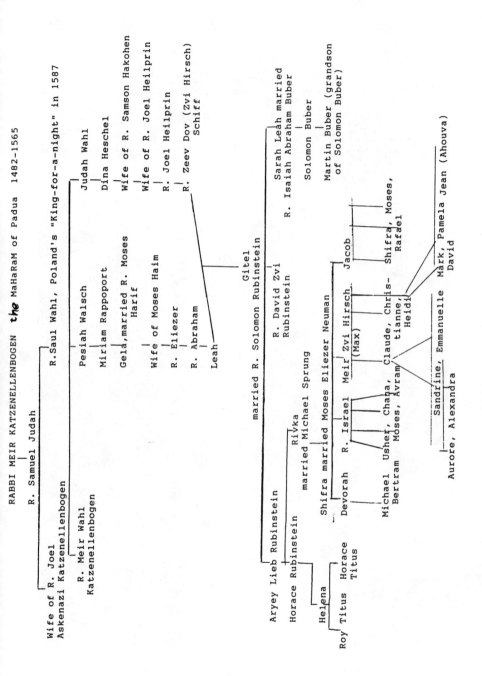

RABBI MEIR KATZENELLENBOGEN *the* MaHaRaM of Padua 1482-1565

Max provided this genealogy

Max at various stages of his life

Max and Claude

Max and Christianne

*Tail gunner with
de Gaul in Brittan*

Max and Shirley Ann

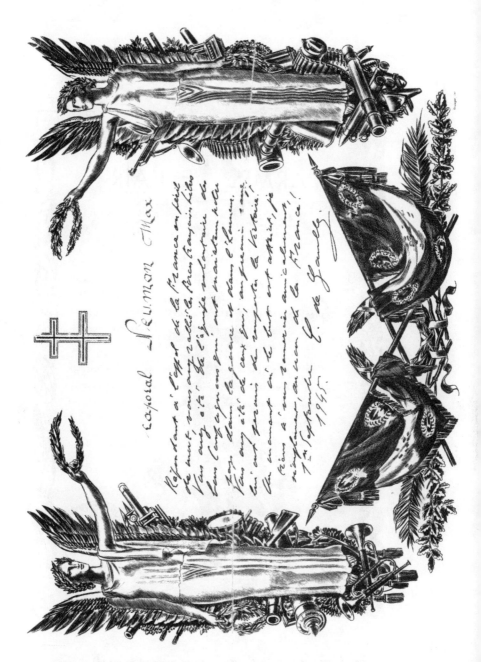

la Croix de Lorraine (one of Max's prized medals)

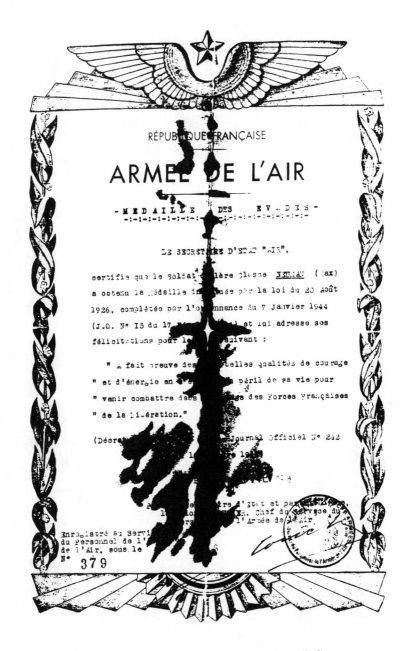

la Medaille des Evades (another prized medal)

14

The Pathos
by Shirley Ann Newman

A good deal of this account of Max Neuman's early life
      deals with his struggle to survive
         the Second World War.

But for many who lived through that ordeal
      —and Max was one of those—
      there appears to be an *inner war*,
         incipient in the womb-life,
its augmentation coinciding with fetal growth:
a pot-boiling thorny mass
         that never dissipates,
         never cools, and—
as the bush that Moses encountered in the
wilderness
         —it burns but is not consumed.

The barbs and bristles of life's experiences agitate,
         inflame,
         goad,
      incite through a continuum of conflict,
         dissonance,
         overt rage,
subsiding into periods of hiatus
only until a period of refreshment
         breeds renewed force
as the barbs resume their grinding
         and churning
         within the convulsed soul
         and mind relentlessly.

In truth, some wars never end!

Chapter One
Introduction

MAX AND HIS GHOSTS

Max was a charmer, everyone said so. He entertained them, he amused them, he flattered them. They loved him. What endeared him to me in part, was that he felt comfortable enough to be "himself" with me when we were alone: often quite "un-charming." Indeed, it was difficult when he was morose, angry, bitter, suspicious, wary, withdrawn, guilt-ridden. But I valued the fact that he trusted me sufficiently to unmask; he trusted no one else to know him in his off-stage, costume-less, make-up-less moments. I felt his pain. I had not caused it, and, sadly, it took too long for me to learn how to alleviate it even slightly. But it did help that my love was steadfast. I tend to believe that on one level it made the unbearable part of his life somewhat more bearable.

Following the trauma of the Second World War, Max began to experience endless nightmares and flashbacks involving hideous episodes. It was in 1983, the last decade of the life of Max Neuman that I said one day, "Those ghosts that tease and taunt you will not ever go away if you keep them locked in a dark closet of your mind. Fling open the door, confront them with a great flood of light. They will surely flinch, recoil from it, and fade off into oblivion. Thus you will free yourself from their tormenting reminders." The great white light I referred to was a symbolic spotlight directed upon the collected memories of traumatic events.

17

Daring to turn it on, to use its power to dis-empower the demons would induce them to retreat.

That is how we came to unfold, unravel, and record three decades of the personal history of Max H. Neuman, a.k.a. Maxwell Herbert Newman.

Toward the end of his days, incapacitated by numerous maladies, he ruefully yielded, surrendering to the inevitability of his total reliance upon my unequivocally loving ministrations that brought comfort and spiritual quiescence to his flickering life force. Then one day, a month before his 82nd birthday, even that last ember was quietly and peacefully extinguished.

I have written of a time I did not know in the way my husband did, of places to which I have either never been or am only barely acquainted with, and of people whose experiences were so different from mine that I feel I am only technically the author of this work. Strictly speaking, I am a conduit through which my husband channeled and transmitted this story, in all its detail to you, the reader. It is as he remembered this period of his life, and as he related it to me. If any deviation in facts exists: names or events it is intentional, explainable only by errors in memory.

Chapter Two
I Cut My Own Cord

In the home of Michael Sprung and Rivka Rubinstein Sprung, their daughter Shifra gave birth to Max and named him Meir Hirsch ben (son of) Moses Eliezer Neuman, her husband, known colloquially as "Moshe." Shifra was the only child of Michael and Rivka, who agreed to the marriage if their daughter and son-in-law would remain for an indeterminate time in the house of her father where she had been born. It was in the city of Lizensk, which was then a thriving Jewish community of the Austro-Hungarian empire. Emperor Franz Joseph was beloved by the Jews because of the latitude they enjoyed as they compared their conditions with those of Russian Jews and many others who lived under harsh, unstable, oppressive regulations.

Max was the third child, preceded by his sister Deborah, six years his senior, and by his brother Israel, three years older than Max. He was a baby of two years when the First World War commenced. His father Moshe was recruited into the army of the Emperor as a chaplain. A principal duty was to supervise the diet of the Jewish soldiers to ensure its conformity to the Jewish restrictive laws of Kashruth. Although posted in Holland, which was a leading provider of the cheese and cured meats purchased for the military, he moved his family to Vienna. There he found a house for Shifra and the three children, and went back and forth from Vienna to Amsterdam to carry out his chaplain's duties, sojourning with his family whenever time permitted.

19

The fourth and last child, Jacob, was born to Shifra and Moshe in their Vienna home in Leopoldstadt, the Jewish quarter of the city. It was a large, commodious house that kept Shifra busy supervising the homemaking. Domestic servants helped her to carry out the duties which included the complex rituals and mandates of Jewish observance, and to look after the children. Dietary-restricted meals, housecleaning, laundry, teaching discipline and manners to the children kept the mistress of the house and her maids well occupied.

Shifra was a tall, slender woman with a proud bearing and nervous energy. She moved about the house efficiently and confidently. She was a firm but gentle woman who knew what her religion expected of her as a wife and as a mother; she was in harmony with her prescribed role. Her children and her husband loved and respected her. The children's behavior was modified without corporal punishment from their mother, nor did she inflict loud, quarrelsome remonstrances. A meaningful glance was often enough to redirect a maverick to the right path. For the era and the environment in which she grew up and lived Shifra was an educated woman. But rigid boundaries limited her sources of learning and impacted upon her attitudes and beliefs. She knew what she needed to know for a religious and refined lifestyle in Jewish-Austrian early twentieth-century culture.

Even under wartime conditions the city of Vienna had a charm and animation that were as tendrils coiling tightly around the emotions of baby Max. The brightly colored street cars that rattled along the tracks with bells clanging, perpetually beckoned the little boy. Their color, sound, and motion were as bewitching as a Lorelei. The child would slip unnoticed from his mother's view while her attention was diverted, and board the transport vehicle as it shivered to a halt to take on waiting passengers. Rapt and eager little Max gazed out of a window, ingesting the scene that changed speedily during these wonderful surreptitious tram car rides. His eyes grew wide, his curls of hair danced and frolicked with the motion of his head and the jolting movement of the vehicle.

The first time the child arrived at the depot, alone except for the motorman who didn't notice his presence until he brought the tram to a final halt, the frantic driver was gripped with alarm and consternation. But when the toddler was led into the office, the man learned that officials had already been alerted to watch for an unaccompanied three year-old boy. When Max made his appearance his mother was notified to come and collect him. While he waited unaware of the furor at home, there at the depot he munched cookies and chocolates the transit workers offered him. Time after time Max repeated this adventure until it became routine for streetcar personnel to notify Frau Neuman to come for the incorrigible little wanderer.

*   *   *

The war ended. The Austro-Hungarian empire which was on the losing side was dismantled. The map of Europe, re-drawn, transformed Lizensk to a city of Poland. Nevertheless the Neuman family rejoined Shifra's parents as had been promised by Moshe Neuman who had been chosen as an eligible bridegroom principally because of his piety and scholarliness but also on condition that Shifra could remain close to her parents. Moshe had acquired valuable and very tempting business connections while in Holland during the war; his plans even advanced to packing all their personal and household goods for moving his wife and four children to Amsterdam, his commitment to the pre-nuptial promise obliged him to abandon the project. However, he did accept an alternative offer, an agency of the Holland-American Steamship Company, requisitioning one of the rooms of the

21

lower floor of the family three story house to use as his office.

Chapter Three
Indications Of My
Inclinations

None of the bewitching excitement of Vienna awaited Max, who was intelligent, inquisitive, and constantly in need of challenge and stimulation. Early on there were new places to explore in Lizensk, also new people to satisfy the child's curiosity, but-soon the rigid orthodox traditions, made even more stringent by the Jewish mores of a smaller community took control of his life. Even the timing of that change was a negative factor: the Neuman family left Vienna at the end of the usually carefree years of a little boy. They came to Lizensk soon after he started school. He thus equated life in Vienna with freedom and unrestriction, and life in Lizensk with stringent and mandated responsibilities. There were long hours of religion school that followed secular school session, as well as what Max viewed as dreary, stern limitations of the Sabbath day. With the immaturity and simplistic analysis of a child he concluded he would have been able to remain in the same delightful stage of *sans souci* if only he had not been uprooted from lovely, lively, lilting Vienna.

The residents of Lizensk, not only the recently arrived Neumans, but so many that returned after temporary displacement during the war years, and even those who had remained in the town, were in a period of adjustment—or perhaps the beginning of prolonged maladjustment. Lizensk had been an Austrian city during the Empire period, with

23

German as its mother tongue. Now it was Polish. Poles from various other parts of Poland moved into Lizensk. Their customs and personalities seemed strange and intrusive; their Slavic language seemed an affront to the German-speaking population. A level of hostility and resentment between the two ethnic groups became apparent. Even among the Jews, some Austrian, some Polish, all of whom spoke Yiddish, the dialects and some of the vocabulary contained differences. Often differences rather than commonalties were stressed and proved to be divisive. The non-Jewish Poles brought with them their historic anti-Semitic attitudes that made the Jews uneasy, for it marked a change from the good relations they enjoyed with their Christian neighbors before the war. It was bewildering even to the gentiles, formerly congenial Austrians.

Many who now found themselves in reduced circumstances were easy converts to the manifestations of hate and prejudice. For some Austrians of both faiths the situation in Lizensk was unsatisfactory and they made the decision to move to the newly-defined Austrian nation. But Max's grandparents, and thus his parents as well, remained rooted to the town, to the family home, and to what remained of their outlying farmland and timber forests after the fall of the Empire.

The lower floor of the house included rooms set aside for the affairs of business of the local bank which was in the charge of Michael Sprung. Max often watched his grandfather open the immense safe before the commencement of the business day. First a key was inserted; this enabled the dials to turn. Grandpa Sprung moved them to right and to left in accordance with the combination of numbers that would permit the huge thick door to swing open on massive hinges that groaned and squeaked with the strain. From time to time his grandfather would hold the key out to Max. The boy felt privileged on these occasions. He would insert the key and

24

then step back as he knew he was expected to do so that his grandfather could cover with his own body the view of the mysterious black dial with its circle of numbers. Max wondered how old he would be before he might be privy to that grave important secret: the combination. The banker activated the cylinders; Max watched as the door slowly swung open.

*   *   *

At school Max understood the lessons quickly, and the teacher's explanations easily. When these lessons were repeated several times for the benefit of slower learners, Max grew bored, restless and inattentive. Fantasies and daydreams moved into his consciousness; the teacher's voice faded into oblivion. At times he conjured up mischief that became acts of class disruption. In the schoolyard during recess he gave vent to his frustrated mind and muscles, engaging in rough-and-tumble that brought punishment upon him from the teacher and later from his parents. His fists were swift and tough; they bloodied the noses of foes even older and weightier than he. Standing up to a local bully one day, Max wielded a blow that forced the older boy's lip between his teeth requiring days of skilled dentistry to release it. One of the worst sieges of punishment from his exasperated and humiliated parents resulted from that confrontation. But never again was the younger boy plagued by the taunting and threats of the neighborhood juvenile terror. From then on it was Max who was feared, but only by those boys who picked on smaller children and upon those frail and timid "yeshiva buchers" indoctrinated with passivity. Max never had much confidence in the religious promise of nebulous afterlife rewards and blessings. He adhered strictly to a philosophy of pay-as-you-go. If you hurt him you paid. He demanded his recompense right here and right now!

More and more he resisted the regimented, stultifying

25

school methods of the era, and whenever possible he slipped away to spend hours watching the fascinations of pharmacy at the local chemist's shop. To his great delight he was often allowed to mix the powders and potions the chemist measured out in the porcelain mixing pots as he filled his customers' prescriptions. To his family's distress Max sometimes accepted tidbits of non-kosher food that were offered him. He was punished for these visits to the Gentile establishment, both for missing school and for breaking the dietary laws of Jewish observance.

The office of the local dentist was another delightful "hangout" for Max. The shiny mysterious equipment was only part of the allure. Of greater interest was the dentist's fascinating scientific knowledge that he was pleased to relate to the intelligent child. He patiently explained all sorts of taboo subjects and ideas that would have remained outside the scope of Max's understanding for many years to come in his sheltered, restricted environment. Max decided he would be a dentist when he grew up, an ambition which was never to be realized.

In athletics Max achieved the recognition, success and self-esteem that the other areas of his life were not earning for him. He was strong, muscular and very quick. He excelled in running competitively and in games such as soccer. Before long his teachers not only allowed, but encouraged him to train for school athletic competitions, at the expense of his academic studies, so as to bring credit and honor to his school in sporting events with other schools in the region. When his homework was left undone and when he came to examinations unprepared, all was forgiven because he was a "star" athlete.

Sports became a consuming interest, thus when Max was punished for playing ball on the Sabbath by confinement to his room, he stealthily left the house via the window. This was discovered; after that his shoes were taken before he was locked in his room. Only then did he submit to what he considered parental tyranny.

*   *   *

The headmaster of the school the boys attended was an excellent administrator. He also actively opposed the swelling tide of anti-Semitism that began to flow into Lizensk from established Polish strongholds and was starting to alarm Jewish students. His son, who lacked the headmaster's benign, refined personality, was the physical education teacher. Bigoted, hostile, and abusive to the passive Jewish boys, disinclined to do well in sports and gymnastics, he often used the switch upon them. Although wielding corporal punishment was a teacher's prerogative, it did have limitations. A teacher was ill-advised to resort to sadistic, damaging blows.

Max's older brother Israel excelled in all areas of academics. Diametrically opposite to Max, he had no aptitude for physical activities. When this teacher grew sufficiently exasperated with Israel one day, and felt frustrated by this highly intelligent but puny boy who could not perform the feats required in gymnastics class, he lunged at him, twisting and tearing at the side locks that bobbed around the cheeks and neck of his student, then beating the terrified boy across his thin bony back. Later that day Israel exhibited to his parents the effects of the lash as he described the indignities to which he had been subjected. The headmaster was appalled and deeply troubled that such an event should take place in his school. All the worse because it was his own son who had perpetrated the vicious and cowardly act. Mr. and Mrs. Neuman promptly withdrew their son from the school and engaged private tutors, declining to send Israel back even after receiving formal apologies from the teacher, the headmaster and the district superintendent of schools.

27

Although three years younger than Israel, and even though he often scuffled with his brother in fraternal conflicts, Max took it upon himself to avenge the offending attack upon a family member. Even as he questioned and doubted Scripture and ritual, the boy selectively internalized some of the Biblical anecdotes and tales that suited his own point of view. A favorite was the account of David and Goliath. He read it carefully and repeatedly, identifying with the young, small, but victorious David who overcame the power of a giant by means of a strong, swift weapon. The boy Max fashioned a magnificent sling shot, which was kept in secret and not used for many months after finishing it. Carefully he carved a fine piece of timber into a "Y," smoothed and oiled it. He recalled seeing maids using a pomade which was kept in the supplies cupboard. The young girls lubricated and massaged the home's wonderful pieces of antique furniture with it. Secretly Max ferreted out this lubricant, spreading and working it into the wood that was to become a sling shot, then returned the product to the closet. From the cobbler he obtained a piece of strong elastic. From his mother's sewing basket he took the stout needle and spool of darning thread he needed to complete the craft. The sling shot and a cache of carefully selected stones were guarded and hidden except during clandestine target practice sessions and when implemented infrequently as an attack weapon. Almost new, rarely used and for only one later act of retribution Max wielded it upon the cruel teacher who had wounded his elder brother and affronted his family.

One day, shortly after Israel had been struck, Max brought the sling shot to school with him. During recess in the school yard he regarded the offending teacher who stood coaching some boys as they played soccer. Max told his friends he was going to the toilet, scaled a fence which separated the yard from a path leading to the outhouses.

Quickly he ran along the path, found a position from which he could see the teacher, but that shielded him from view. He took careful aim. With the largest, flintiest stone cradled in the leather, Max drew back on the elastic bands until they were taut. The distance between him and the teacher was great, but so powerful was the weapon and its ammunition, so precise the boy's aim and so driven by a thirst for revenge was the nine-year-old schoolboy that the stone struck the shoulder blade of the teacher like a bullet.

Almost as fleet as the attacking stone was Max's retreat; backtracking the path, he then leapt over the fence and returned to his classmates. Everyone was hurrying toward the howling wounded gym teacher. Max relates: "'What happened, what's all the tumult?' I skillfully feigned innocence as I hurled my question into the excited mass of students. A red haired boy, his face flushed, sputtered excitedly, 'I think Mr. Granick got shot.' 'Are you crazy?' hooted the boy next to him. 'The war's over, you idiot. I think a fast ball hit him real hard.'"

While under treatment in hospital and then convalescing at home, the teacher gave interviews to the police and to school authorities. Investigations and interrogations proved futile:

"I was never revealed as the culprit. But I agonized over the possibilities and reluctantly concluded that in my own best interest the sling shot must never be used again. And it wasn't, except for one subsequent occasion when I ferreted it out of retirement to avenge my younger brother Jacob.

"After the incident in the schoolyard I worried through the school day, fearing the slingshot would be discovered beneath my flannel shirt where I concealed it. When the dismissal bell rang I felt safe. I raced home, up to my room which was in the attic. 'Come have some bread and jam,' My grandmother sang out to my back as I hurried past her in the kitchen. 'In a minute, Bubbie.' I stood uncertainly in the

middle of my room considering possible safe places for my weapon. No corner, no drawer, no shelf might not be approached by a maid while dusting, polishing, straightening up. Nor by my mother, who brought my laundered, folded clothes to my room and put them away after every wash day. No, it had to be placed somewhere outside of the room. I remembered a jutting nail outside the window ledge. I stuffed the slingshot into a heavy sock, then put the second sock of the pair around the first. A single sock in the drawer might arouse curiosity, I reasoned. A piece of string was tied around the small bundle, which was then hooked on to the nail. No one would see the brown wad because of the density of a large oak tree in the yard below my window, whose branches would hide it. I went back downstairs, washed my hands dutifully, recited the required blessing and ate the bread spread with quince jam while Bubbie ran a wrinkled hand through my hair and then kissed the top of my head. 'Siess punim,' sweet face, she murmured lovingly as she turned back to her cooking."

Not only active participation in sports, but all of outdoor life held a passionate attraction for Max. He was always eager to ride through the countryside with his grandfather when invited to join him as he went on business to the family's tenant-farmed lands beyond the city. For generations the family of Michael Sprung had owned acreage that yielded crops and timber. These were produced and sold on a shared basis with the families that lived and worked on the land. In the cold mountain air of the Carpathians tall, strong trees grew, hearty grains and cold-weather fruits flourished and were harvested. Max felt a release and exhilaration as he and his grandfather sped in the horse-drawn carriage through fields and woods. The youngster stood up, holding the reins, excited and happy, not realizing that at his back it was really *Zeidah* Grandpa controlling the animals. Forever after he retained this affinity to the out-of-doors.

However, he never did he develop a positive relationship to the family's fundamentalist Judaism. Nor would Max fall

30

under the spell of such fearsome—and to him—implausible requirements such as one which forbade viewing the *bimah*, the platform that held the ark and scrolls, from which eyes were to be averted during the recitation of the benediction by the *Kohane*, the High Priest, authorized to recite this special prayer. Max's father had an enormous woolen prayer shawl; the *tallit* enabled the pious man to enfold his two younger sons, Max and Jacob while the benediction was recited. Father, with one son on either side of him were wrapped in the great woolen shawl, with the heads of the little boys covered. This was to prevent them from looking at the procedure, a consequence, children were cautioned was to risk blindness. One day Max could no longer contain his curiosity, coupled with his incredulity; he decided to take the chance. Beneath the creamy soft folds of the *tallit* he took a pin from his pocket and furtively pricked a hole large enough to peer through. His lack of belief was confirmed when his sight remained unimpaired. Skepticism grew unchecked, rampant from then on.

Before long the hole in the *tallit* was discovered; Max's parents speculated about its source, mildly questioning whether he was the culprit. When he denied culpability the issue was dropped. "It was probably a moth hole," his father concluded conciliatorially. In accordance with ethical Judaism, one must not condemn if there is any doubt of the guilt of a suspect.

The boy appeared to know how far he wanted to go in his risk-taking, as when he decided to give up the use of his sling shot. He had peered at the Kohanim during a benediction, a sin said to be punishable by blindness, but he would not unduly tempt fate. He dared not cause a Torah scroll to fall to the floor, an act, he was warned, which *could* result in death. The young doubter did place limits upon his tests.

Every afternoon when public school session ended the

31

young Jewish boys went off to *cheder*. Their religious studies included reading and writing in the language of the Hebrew scriptures. They learned laws, commandments, customs, and history, but never with any attempt on the part of the teacher to stimulate interest and imagination, or to rationalize the philosophical issues that might be open to question by the intellectually dubious or curious. Contradictions and ambiguities were glossed over. Max asked questions. The answers were swift and final: they were sharp blows to his head and face. The only verbal replies were: "That's the way it is written; just listen and do what you are told." He did not stop believing; he just never learned to believe, in the first place.

The teacher was a harsh angry man who held his young students in an iron grip of fear and antipathy. Nevertheless the rebellious Max found outlets for the distasteful atmosphere. He stayed away whenever he could; when he was present he resorted to acts of mischief that frustrated and tormented the "rebbe" but brought comic relief to the mutually trapped youngsters.

One mild sunny day Max watched a fly enter the open classroom window. Usually when that happened the teacher would reach for his fly swatter as the poor unsuspecting little creature buzzed near his desk. Swat, and the pest was doomed. Pupils, too, were to rid the room of the annoying insects. This day the teacher was absorbed in the lesson or otherwise distracted, and ignored the fly for the moment or failed to become aware of its presence. Neither did he appear to observe the fly drifting out the window from which it had entered. Max rose from his seat, walked to the teacher's desk, took the fly swatter and batted it smartly across the teacher's forehead. Stunned by the impact and the insolent gesture, the man let out a roar of outrage and indignation. He lunged at the boy who was by then sauntering to his seat. Max turned, raised his palms upward in a gesture of innocence as he protested: "But rebbe, there was a fly on your forehead." The teacher, dubious but disconcerted by the explanation, fell silent and did not mete out the usual punishment for misconduct: the sharp stinging blows on a boy's open palm as it was struck with the teacher's desk ruler.

Not only were disciplinary problems dealt with in this manner, but they were a consequence to boys who did not grasp rapidly enough—or thoroughly enough—the lesson at hand. A ruler across the hand was wielded at will for not fulfilling the mandate of absolute silence and a statue-like posture while the teacher delivered his lesson in a dreary and often obscure manner.

Adult males found diversion in card games. But for the boys a deck of cards was unobtainable from their fathers. Max was able to have a well-worn deck of playing cards from the pharmacist who had grown to be his friend. The word went around that Max was conducting a card game, at a designated time, in the balcony of the synagogue. He and a few of the most daring cheder students absented themselves during recess one day and met in the upstairs pews that were reserved for the women of the congregation but never occupied during the weekdays. The men were busy and noisy as they conducted their sundown prayers, and the boys went unnoticed because the panels that kept the women discretely hidden from men's view also concealed the mischievous boys. They spoke in whispers and these were not heard above the din of the men at prayer. The "house" was represented by Max. Each boy put a small coin into the "pot." Max took one of the coins for himself and the rest went to the winner of the card game, a simplified form of poker. After the first game was carried out successfully there were always boys ready to spread the word to meet in the same obscure place at the time Max scheduled and which coincided with the hour the synagogue would be open and occupied by at least ten men. As with all crimes, luck often deserts the perpetrators and one day the gamblers were discovered. The ringleader Max was escorted home by his angry, exasperated father, who gave him one of the severest thrashings of his boyhood.

*   *   *

The cheder's rebbe was paid a pittance in tuition by his students' parents. He was a married man, with children of his own, and he could barely subsist by teaching every available child whose parents could afford the small fee. After becoming a bar mitzvah Israel was enrolled in the Warsaw yeshiva, a seminary that took only highly qualified boys that showed great promise. That left just Max and Jacob to continue attending the local cheder. Jacob and his classmates, little fellows of six and seven years, received their instruction while the older boys were at recess. One day Max was distracted from the game he was playing during his recess period; he saw the rebbe scold and spank his little brother. Jacob was wailing and teary-eyed, and Max felt his anger welling up to a rolling boil. The next day, armed with the sling shot that had previously been laid to rest, Max covertly took aim and shattered a window of the school room. He knew the poor teacher would have to replace it out of his meager earnings if no guilty party could be found to make compensation. Max was not found out, and resentment over his small brother's punishment, thus vindicated, subsided.

Overburdened but unwilling to decline to take any new students that applied for tutelage the rebbe proposed that some of the older, brighter students act as teacher's assistants. Max met the teacher's plan with impudence: "How much will you pay me, Rebbe?" The rebbe shrugged him off angrily. Max went on: "You are paid to teach us, Rebbe, so you must give us something if we do part of your job." He turned to the few boys who had been singled out as good students capable

34

of helping the little ones. "Don't do it unless he pays us," Max ordered the boys who so often found themselves responding obediently to the strong leadership personality of the middle Neuman son.

About a week later Shifra, whose function it was to deal with such matters as arrangements for the children's education, came to the cheder to pay the tuition for the coming semester. The rebbe received her courteously and with dignity, as always. He took his account book and told her how much she owed him. "It will be a saving to you, Mrs. Neuman, now that you have to pay for only your little Jacob." Puzzled, Max's mother tactfully sought to correct him. "But Rebbe, there is Max to pay for as well." The teacher flushed darkly and his hands trembled as he set down his book and faced the confused mother. "Not Max! I will not any longer have your son in my school." His voice cracked with the effort of controlling his anger. "He is a union organizer instigating a strike of my best students against me. That little *momser* is not a student of mine from now on."

Shifra listened to the tale of Max's demand for payment to help the younger students, and how he incited the rebellion among other boys. Barely able to contain her amusement, she paid the fee for Jacob, and hurried home to relate the anecdote to her husband, where they both burst into gales of laughter. Moses, feigning sternness between loud guffaws beckoned Max, bent his son "bottom up" across his knees and gave the boy a mock thrashing. After that the youthful rebel was tutored at home and prepared for his bar mitzvah.

*   *   *

Besides the large downstairs room of the Sprung-Neuman home which was utilized for the banking enterprise of Michael Sprung, another, somewhat smaller one, was turned into the office for Moses Neuman to use as his agency of the Holland-American Steamship Lines. Though keenly disappointed about giving up his opportunity to move his family to Amsterdam, he cheerfully set about developing a clientele in Lizensk

The talents of Moses Eliezar Neuman extended well beyond the areas of religion and philosophy. He knew the English language, an important requisite for running the agency, which was involved in transporting people from Europe to America. People of Lizensk and nearby cities often came with a letter in English from a cousin or brother or family friend in America. Moses would read aloud the contents of the letter, translating it into Yiddish, Polish or German as the eager recipient listened to descriptions of the wonderful possibilities for a prosperous life in the New World, and the sometimes discreet references to the lack of social and ritual restraints in this modern country. Neuman arranged the papers and the details of passage, finally issuing a *shiffskarte*—a ticket for a vessel sailing to New York.

The little son, Max, often lingered in the office listening as his father and a client spoke of this great land across the Atlantic Ocean. He burned and ached to see more of the world than this small city and its surroundings. Soon he planned the first step in his project: to run off and join his older brother who was at school in Warsaw. Warsaw was not New York, to be sure, but it was a large city, a metropolis, that would satisfy him for a start. Taking little else than some coins he had managed to save, Max walked to the railroad station. He bought a ticket, but before the train arrived Max saw the figure of his father hurrying toward him. With little fuss but great firmness Moses hustled the ten year old runaway back home. Max made another attempt not long after that aborted one. This time he walked about ten kilometers to the next station before he boarded the train to Warsaw. Thus, unannounced he presented himself at the home in which Israel was taking his board and lodging while attending classes at the *Yeshiva*, the religion seminary.

His older brother was as different from Max as day is from night. Israel, with undiluted religious belief and accord, conformed unequivocally to the approved traditions. At the *Yeshiva* he was studiously entrenched in the honored engagement with the Talmud, the Mishna, and all the other wonders and complexities that surrounded a Hebrew scholar whose sights were set upon the Doctorate he ultimately acquired after years in Warsaw and later in Berlin. At first Israel expressed delight at the appearance of his younger brother in this unexpected arrival. Then he grew angry when he heard that Max had come unbeknownst to anyone, for he realized how distraught their parents must be over the boy's disappearance. He slapped Max across the cheek as he lectured him. Max heard words like "honor," "duty," "gratitude," as the blows stung and reddened his face. Israel hurried off to the telegraph office to allay the parents' undoubted anxiety.

When he came back he listened to Max's declaration that he would run away and disappear if he were not allowed to stay in Warsaw, at least for awhile. Israel communicated with his parents again. Following the consultation Israel arranged for Max to be admitted to a boys' religious boarding school. But after six weeks Max rejected this situation and pleaded to be sent to Mielec, the city of the home of the boys' paternal grandparents. After another discussion over the issue it was agreed Max could go there for awhile, until—it was hoped—his restlessness subsided.

"I was enrolled in a day school and attended with fair regularity for one semester. After school I liked to go to the small but well-stocked bookstore owned by my "Zeidah"(Grandpa) Neuman. For many hours each day, in the late afternoons I moved among the aisles of shelves, selecting a volume on some subject wondrous and new to me;

I read hungrily, voraciously: ingesting, absorbing, assimilating as much as I could and as quickly as I could." For most of his life Max expanded his limited formal education with books, newspapers and magazines, particularly in the fields of history, geography, politics, and world affairs.

After six months Max's mother and his sister Deborah, eldest of the four Neuman children went to Mielec to fetch the boy. It was then Max learned that during his absence his grandfather Michael Sprung had suffered an illness to which he succumbed. Max returned home to find his grandmother sad and quiet, but apparently comforted to have her wayward grandson back with her. Sheepishly Max endured the elderly woman's stern and disapproving gaze as she noted he had trimmed off his *payot*, ear curls. The bereaved widow was devoid of her former spirited responses and did not verbally raise the issue. From the time he began to go to school Max had formed the habit of tucking the long ringlets behind his ears and beneath his skullcap, the *kipah*. After being chided for doing this he appeared from his room one morning with one of the curls cut off. He received a beating for the act of defiance but his parents concluded it was just as well to allow him to conceal this object of distinctiveness rather than have him resort to removing the locks. Far from home, in Mielec he had cut them off, returning home without them. Soon they grew back.

Almost as soon as he returned Max announced his firm intention to stay at home only until after he became a bar mitzvah. The rite of passage in the Hebrew religion, occurs at thirteen years; males reached the age of adult responsibility for their actions (twelve-and-a-half for females), and demonstrate at the synagogue, in the presence of members of the congregation their understanding of the body of laws, as well as the ability to read and write in Hebrew—the language of the Bible, and other holy books and documents. This life-cycle event, when a boy becomes a "son of the commandment," is so significant that even maverick Max conceded it was just as well to remain with his family for the celebration of the event. It was still three years away when Max was brought back to Lizensk; his parents and grandmother were confident he would mature sufficiently by then to forget such childish nonsense.

Despite their conviction, the boy's projected plans took on reality in his own mind as his thirteenth birthday, marked by the bar mitzvah celebration, came and passed.

Although Max lacked commitment to the beliefs and rituals of the Hebrew religion the ten years of mandated studies were tolerated to satisfy his father. He went through the rite in the presence of his family, friends, the synagogue congregation, and anyone who cared to witness the momentous occasion. Max earned for _Reb Moshe_ the nods and smiles of approval from the other "pillars of the Jewish community" as he read from the Torah: the Pentateuch, recited the _Haftarah_: the Prophets, and delivered his own interpretations with remarkable ability. "Reb Moshe"—the unofficial title of Moses Neuman, because of his scholarship and piety—noted his son's performance with carefully concealed pride. In the afternoon, following the service at the synagogue, there was an elegant reception in the huge ballroom which occupied the entire second story of the Sprung-Neuman house. The highly polished hardwood floor had been buffed to a mirror gloss, the banquet table—meters long and laid with snow white embroidered linen napery—was heaped with exquisite comestibles on silver and fine porcelain platters. At the appointed time hordes of local and out-of-town guests filled the enormous chamber for the festive meal. With the pressure of the religious ceremony behind him, Max devoted himself to socializing with his friends and cousins. He and the other youngsters made countless trips back to the buffet for the dazzling delights of the palate. After many hours the local guests departed but family members, who had voyaged from Vienna, Gratz, Berlin, Hannover, Crakow, and Warsaw remained for the next few days. Formal and traditional sleeping arrangements had to be abandoned. People were bedded down in any way possible.

Gradually the relatives drifted off and when life returned to routine the "man-boy" redoubled his preoccupation with a plan to leave home. It was not until a few months passed, when the harsh months of winter yielded to the benignity of springtime that Max severed the cord that bound him to his family's control.

During those last few months after becoming a bar mitzvah, Max was required to do daily morning prayers at the House of Prayer, as did all adult Jewish males of religious conviction or who complied out of a reluctance to defy communal mores. Not being religious, he was nonetheless not allowed to come to the breakfast table until after his mother was assured he had attended morning worship. "Show me your arm," his mother commanded, inspecting for the pressure marks made by the narrow leather straps, the prayer tapes known as *tefillin*, wound in a set pattern. Soon Max began showing the trusting woman the marks of a strap he devised to wear during the hour he was out of the house playing ball instead of praying. (Deuteronomy 6:6-8 contains the admonition to bind the words of God upon one's body.)

Max regarded the prayers and rituals imposed upon him as a tyranny, an unreasonable display of adult power bent on denying him the expression of his natural inclinations and desires. The traditions, even those that included the merriment of music and holiday games, and delectable foods, he superciliously attributed to mindless habit born of long-standing repetition that deliberately ignored forward-looking change. Even while enjoying family and community festivity, Max kept focused on his resentment. He believed he was being pressed into a mold of a shape different from his personal contours. At eleven, twelve, thirteen years old Max Neuman was not about to defer to these "frozen-in-time" adults!

Long past youth and well into middle-age the memories of warm, happy aspects of his early life finally, gradually, and timidly crept back, confusing his emotions with their startling intrusion. The festival days grew increasingly poignant by recollections of those early years with his family.

Just before the annual Passover season there was a procedure in which Max, the boy was allowed to participate. It was when the men of the strictly observant families gathered at the bakery to prepare an especially sacred form of the usual unleavened bread, known as the *shmurer matzot,* as distinguished from the quantity of ordinary Passover matzot each family buys to replace the leavened bread used throughout the rest of the year. A small spiked wheel used to perforate the squares of matzot was given to the boys who accompanied their fathers to this baking session. One year, when he was eight years old and finding it a bit uninteresting to form the straight parallel lines of tiny holes, Max thought of a more innovative approach. He began to move and guide the wheel in curves and circles, sketching the naked torsos of females, complete with nippled breasts. Fortunately these pious men, busy with their own baking functions never noticed the child's artistic creations. Max never had any idea whose seder tables his handiwork graced—or more accurately—disgraced!

An important part of Max's life "in the nest" that came to conclusion when he went away was the unequivocal favor he enjoyed with Rivka Rubinstein Sprung, his matriarchal grandmother. Even Max's father seldom found the courage to scold or punish the youngster in the presence of this devoted

41

champion. Whenever Max assessed his situation as one of "grave peril" all he had to do as a small boy was to retreat beneath the long billowing folds of *Bubbie's* skirt. She would raise her arms against the pursuer in a gesture of "out of bounds" and the would-be punisher did not dare try to wrest him from this refuge.

Max also found great favor with his sister Deborah, six years his senior, beautiful and accomplished. Secretly, despite parental disapproval of the frivolity of modern dancing for young boys, Max learned at Deborah's instruction the delights of waltzing. She and he moved rhythmically to the lovely Viennese music that the two hummed as Deborah guided her little brother through the graceful steps of the day's popular dance. He was her chaperone, too, when she was permitted to attend Sunday afternoon tea dances for young people. Although charged with the responsibility of safeguarding his sister Deborah's virtue he busied himself teasing and furtively pinching the smaller girls who had also come with older sisters.

Young girls could not be expected to—nor allowed to—master the profundities of scholarly books, but had permission to enjoy the delights of music and other aesthetic pursuits. Deborah played the violin and piano, often providing the after-Shabbat musicales for the family and guests.

Moses Neuman, appreciative recipient of Talmudic enrichment, also enjoyed such cultural gifts as languages and music. Often it was he who played he violin for the parlor recitals, with Deborah at the piano. The father gently coaxed the delicate violin to emit soft and plaintive tones or merry heart-lifting melodies, which gave beauty and relaxation to many family evenings. These were among the treasures of his family life sacrificed upon the alters of freedom and modernity when Max left home.

Later remembered too, were Max's nostalgic impressions of the wonders and glories of the huge kitchen with its great wood burning cook stove. The sweet taste and smell of cinnamon and _marzipan_, the yeasty breads, aromas of exotic spices wafting from the steaming medley of paprika, bay leaf, garlic, peppercorns, nutmeg and clove that settled over the house during meal preparations and baking sessions.

Early Friday morning was the time to prepare the Shabbat _cholent_. This was the special potted meat readied in the home kitchen and then carried to the baker's shop and placed in the huge oven, there to simmer, along with the cholent of many other town dwellers until it slowly, thoroughly cooked and remained hot for the Shabbat lunch. Thus the family did not have to endure a cold meal despite the religious prohibition against lighting a fire on the Sabbath. Max was always the proud courier who bore the heavy enamel vessel with its exquisite viand to the baker's on Friday, and then home again just before the Saturday luncheon.

These days of countless childhood experiences became forever irretrievable with passage of time, the changes wrought by the Second World War, the death of his family by the hand of the Nazis. Long after this, Max was able to recall their beauty and their richness, and the merriment of his impish exploits even when parental punishment resulted. At age thirteen life seemed filled with obstructions and confinements to be thrust off like tightly-laced shoes.

For more than three years, from the time he was ten, never did the boy waiver in his resolve to leave the life for which he felt unsuited. He pondered possible means of obtaining a bit of money for emergency use during his flight. This was to ensure he would not be remanded to his parents again should his resourcefulness and guile prove insufficient to obtain essential sustenance before he could support himself. At school Max learned bookbinding skills and he readily found a students' job during hours for which he did not have to account. But these young bookbinders, who were both apprentices and workers had to provide the materials they used. Max charged these to his father, and, as a result, his secret was very soon found out. Moses wielded the belt unstintingly as a punishment for disgracing the family by having taken a job with a tradesman, something done only by sons of the lower classes, or among non-Jews.

Not long after this conflict Moses Neuman had to leave home for a few weeks. Although it was a business trip he was accompanied by his wife. With both his parents absent and Max in the charge of his doting grandmother, the boy behaved even more brazenly. He played truant from school and went to work as a hod carrier, earning what he delightedly deemed to be a fortune. From the mound of bricks alongside a building site he kept up the supply of bricks to the bricklayer to whom he was assigned. The young assistants were paid according to the number of bricks they hauled from the mound to the fellow laying them. Though strong and muscular the thirteen year old boy found the labor arduous. The other boys were considerably older than he, for the minimum age was sixteen. Max was most likely the only applicant who had lied about how old he was, from his assessment of the size and maturity of the other boys on the site. One of the maids of the household, passing by and noticing him, hurried to inform his grandmother. When Max saw the indignant Bubbie Rivka as she came to take him home from such an unsuitable endeavor he fled, well aware of the perilous situation into which he had placed himself. Rivka returned home, confident she need wait only until her wayward grandson felt the pangs of an empty stomach. She was right. When he arrived at dusk he received a stinging paddling, but followed by a good hot meal. The misdeed was

44

reported to his parents upon their return. Grandmother petitioned for no further punishment to the culprit, arguing that she had already meted out a sufficiency. Her sense of justice inclined her to defend the boy against "double jeopardy." Max had the feeling that among the adults, beneath all this outrage over such unseemly activity there was an undercurrent of admiration for his enterprise and drive.

The spring that followed his thirteenth birthday marked the conclusion of Max's boyhood and his life in Lizensk. He never returned even for a visit until 1969. In that year he made a sorrowful and penitent pilgrimage to the city of his ancestors. It was the city in which his parents and his mother's mother, along with other Jewish inhabitants who could not flee to Russia to escape the genocidal edict of the German Third Reich—the invaders of Poland—met death by mass execution, and burial in a mass grave, a trench in the countryside.

Chapter Four
Stop The World:
I Want To Get On!

In 1925 Max could not foresee such horror. The freedom and exquisite enticement of the larger world captivated his thoughts and he gave substance to the phantom dream. He slipped away one morning, carrying with him little more than the small nest egg he had fashioned, the money he had earned for bookbinding and carrying bricks. Remembering it was more prudent to take the train at a station where he would not be recognized, the runaway walked to Rszeszow. This time he did not buy a ticket. He was traveling to Vienna for which the fare would cost more than he could spare out of his meager savings. As the train pulled into the station he boarded with several other passengers.

"The plaintive wail of the train's whistle pierced my soul as I crouched, hidden from the station master and the four passengers waiting to board the night train to Vienna. I shuddered with the anxiety and anticipation of the unknown. Soon the beam of light, competing with the full moon that shone that night heralded the train's arrival. The tracks groaned and creaked. The station master came out of the white wooden building that housed the ticket office and the telegraphic equipment. Mr. Korelski swung his red lantern. The passengers waiting to board the train moved forward so as to be in position to climb the steps when the train came to a halt at the station.

"I watched their every movement, stealthily, cat-like, planning my strategy as I remained well-concealed in the shadow of the station

building. Two of the passengers, a man and a woman who appeared to be traveling together—probably a husband and wife—each had a small valise. There were two other men that were pushing and tugging at oversized cases. At once I decided that these men—not tall, but rather corpulent—and their large luggage afforded enough bulk to conceal me. As the train stopped, and a split second before the first of these men followed the heavy case he had swung upon the steps, I streaked forward, lunging for the train with my side curls flapping like an angel's wings, and my right hand planted atop my head to keep my velvet skullcap from sailing off into the night. I knew I had made a safe maneuver when I noted the station master gallantly occupied in assisting the lady passenger by carrying her valise. Once on board I made a swift right turn, moved to the end of the and slipped into the unoccupied toilet. I locked the door and leaned against it. I scarcely moved until my breath, first coming in rapid short gasps slowed again, and until my burning cheeks cooled as the night air came through the open toilet window fanned them. I felt a trickle of moisture run down the side of my face into my shirt collar. I blotted it with my hand. Convulsively the train lurched forward, then backward, then forward. It stopped, then steadily departed the station, picking up speed as it left behind buildings, farms, then moved swiftly past my own home town of Lizensk along with my family, my friends, my early life. I didn't know forty-four years would pass before a return: that 1969 painful pilgrimage to the silent remnant of the Nazi annihilation of my people and my past."

Max found a compartment where a kindly-looking couple was seated; he sat down on the bench facing them. The woman smiled to him and he felt encouraged. Right after this friendly gesture Max began an appeal to the compassion of these fellow passengers. He said he was desperately anxious to go to Vienna to visit his grandparents who were quite infirm but that, alas, the fare was beyond his possibilities. As he hoped, the couple sympathized with his plight. The man went into the next compartment where two friends of his were traveling. He related the tale of this devoted grandson. The men moved to Max's compartment and all four adults made a shield of their legs to conceal the boy who crouched beneath the bench. In that manner he made the journey, burrowing out of sight each time the conductor came through the cars to check and punch the tickets; also during the border inspections as the train crossed from Poland to Czechoslovakia, then Austria. At other times during the trip Max sat among the four adults who treated him generously from their food hampers.

It was necessary for each of the passengers to present a ticket upon leaving the station at the destination. At the stop before arriving to Vienna, one of the men who shared the conspiracy of Max's illegal passage descended the train during the minutes it waited to dislodge and take on other passengers; he surrendered his ticket as he went out the gate, and bought two tickets for the very short distance to the end of the journey. One was for Max to use when he was leaving the train and had to pass the agent who collected the tickets for exiting the Vienna station.   Good-byes were exchanged. Max expressed his gratitude and hurried away, swallowed up by the lively streets he remembered and loved. With little difficulty he found Leopoldstadt, the neighborhood populated by mostly Jewish families. Generous helpers showed him how to telephone his mother's cousin in the nearby town of Gratz. Rivka Burstein, her husband, and their children had not returned to Lizensk after the first World War, when it became a Polish city. But close family ties remained and Max was certain he would be helped by this branch of the Sprung family that now lived in Austrian Gratz.

The eldest son of Rivka Burstein set out by train from Gratz to Vienna to meet Max. During the telephone conversation Max made it clear he wanted to stay in the capital city, Vienna, so it was with the aid of his cousin that the boy found living quarters with Rivka's husband's relatives there. Soon it was apparent to Max that his emancipation was severely limited by these close family contacts. The family that gave him this temporary room and board arrangement as a friendly accommodation, also took on the supervision of his religious practices, he was reproached for his tendency to overlook them, and sent continual reports to his parents who—even at a distance—issued edicts and mandates he had hoped to escape. Secular school attendance, as well as doing his prayers and studying the Talmud: the deeply philosophical writings of thousands of years of great scholars, all were willfully resisted. For a few weeks, because there was no immediate option, Max endured the regimen.

During that period, he tried to enlist the services of the Jewish organization that was assisting Europeans who wanted to immigrate to America. He sought to have a trip to the United States financed in this manner, and to obtain a "stateless person's" passport. These were being issued by the government of Sweden to people genuinely classified as political refugees. Max knew that young men of military age were fleeing Poland, and claiming refuge on the grounds of not wanting to serve in the army of their "conquerors," as the former Austrians called the Polish government.

The interviewer could barely contain his laughter when this boy earnestly stated he had run away from Poland to avoid the draft. Although well developed for his nearly fourteen years, Max did not succeed in convincing the fatherly man facing him across the desk that he was sixteen. Because of the lack of urgency in his case and not having any responsible relative in America to sign affidavits on his behalf, there would be perhaps a six month wait before the organization arranged passage and documents for him.

This long wait was out of the question for the impatient youngster. He made his own plan, one which was outside legal sanction. His first step was to move on to Italy where that country's several port cities were points of departure for tens of thousands of Europe's emigres looking toward America for a better life.

Leaving Vienna after about seven weeks, Max went to Gratz, to the home of the cousins Burstein. Rivka, who was Shifra's cousin, spoke of the devotion between the two women, and she clearly understood the incompatibility between Austrians and Poles and how difficult it must be to live in Lizensk since the war. Neither Rivka nor Max broached the subject of religious stringency as the reason Max's determination to leave home.

Everyone in Gratz was aware that in the mountain town of nearby Treviso many undocumented persons crossed illegally into Italy, walking along winding footpaths and heavily wooded trails after nightfall. This was the route the Bursteins advocated for their relative who had no official papers other than an officially stamped school identification card, complete with photograph.

Max set out from Gratz, traveled to Klagenfurt, then to Treviso. Others were en route and Max found himself in company and intrepid. Once across to the Italian side he took a train to Trieste. A bustling multi-cultural city, it had a substantial Jewish population. Finding a store with a prominent "Kosher" sign, Max made his first contact. There he was informed of the location of the Polish consulate which he would petition for a passport.

How had he left Poland without one? he was asked. Innocently he claimed there must have been an oversight at the border and that somehow no controller had requested any official document during the busy period during which he had come to Vienna. The story was a bit transparent but the consular official conceded that the boy would need the passport and a ticket home, too, in order to return to his family. He declared himself a stranded Polish national and claimed entitlement to the travel document and a railroad ticket. The consul promptly issued these. Armed with the precious passport, Max had no intention of boarding the train back to Poland.

Max went again to the quarter where Jews of many nationalities—though of few material resources—were crammed into decaying flats and rooming houses. These poor people graciously shared the little they had, and he found his belly well filled with pasta covered with rich tangy sauces. Nor was it difficult to have offers of a bed. Advice was even more freely given.

Max was helped to redeem the train ticket the consul had issued to him. The refunded ticket money along with the small supplement for food that was included constituted the sum total of his resources. He managed to retain most of it through the next adventurous weeks during which he made his attempt to crash the glittering gates of the United States of America.

The cooperative friends he made in Trieste led him to the waterfront from which ships transported people bound for the New World. "Don't try to board the gangplank reserved for passengers in first and second class," he was cautioned. Max did as he was told and noted another gangplank where there was less order and quiet; contrarily, chaos characterized the situation at boarding time as the steerage passengers bundled on to the vessel. Pier, gangway, decks, passageways were swarming with passengers, visitors, members of the crew, and baggage handlers. Cloaked by the activity and confusion Max boarded the ship but did not leave when the horns and loud speaker announcements warned all unauthorized persons to debark. Skillfully he assessed the passengers by looking for pleasant, kindly faces.

After the ship sailed, a few of the Jewish families were

taken into his confidence. For days they aided and abetted his illegal presence, knowing he was spending his nights in a lifeboat and taking his meals in the children's dining salon where one could sit at any table, unlike the adult dining arrangements which had assigned places for the voyage. During the mornings and afternoons there were on-deck tea services, thus there was no shortage of nourishment for the stowaway.

When well out on the high seas one of the ship's officers became aware of this teenage boy who did not appear to have a family attachment, who was clad always the same, in garments that had grown soiled and disheveled. Max was brought to the captain's office, questioned and obliged to admit to being aboard without a ticket. A radiogram was sent to the immigration authorities who waited to take him into custody when the ship arrived at Ellis Island, where one gained entry into the United States or was barred from doing so. Since he was a Jewish lad he was referred to *HIAS*, the Hebrew Immigrants' Aid Society for assistance with arrangements for his return voyage. With alacrity Max's parents wired the money for his passage home and he was escorted to a ship returning to Trieste. This time he had a cabin and all the accommodations and facilities for a delightful sea journey. He not only had a wonderful time but also the sympathy of passengers and crew who thought it was pretty mean of the Americans to make a big fuss about one little boy who wanted to live in their country. "What harm would it do," said one sailor, to let in one extra little boy?" "Those Americans," commented another, "they make a big issue out of nothing!" This was the consensus among passengers as well; Max concurred completely with their indignation. The center of attention, the shipboard's spoiled darling, he had one of the several memorable ocean voyages of his life.

The ship, belonging to Lloyd Triestino Lines arrived back at Trieste. In the company of the assistant purser Max was taken to the Polish Consulate. Speaking in Italian the purser explained the purpose of their presence. "What are you telling him?" Max inquired in German. The purser replied also in German, explaining that he reported Max as a visitor to the ship who had failed to find his way to the gangplank in time to disembark before the sailing. He had come to bid "good-bye" to acquaintances and when the voyage was underway had revealed himself, demanding to return home. Not only to protect the boy had such a story been contrived, but also because the ship's officers feared a reprimand from the company and from government authorities for not having ensured the validity of each person on board the vessel. The mission of getting rid of Max, "the nuisance" was completed. The escorting officer bade farewell to the rascal by urging him to please find another steamship line should he ever again feel the desire for a free ocean voyage. "There are lots of ships leaving from Genoa, too," he recommended as he hastened out of the consulate, "ships of many companies." Left alone with the consul's secretary Max was loudly scolded before he was dismissed after he was again aided with a ticket to return home, as well as a supplement to provide himself with food for the trip. Rogue that he had proved himself to be, he had sailed off to America, returned, and now had the arrogance to request an additional subsidy! "Go, go!" Seek any further help you may need from the organization of your own people, the Jewish benevolent society here in Trieste," Max was advised as a parting suggestion. Unabashed and undaunted he sauntered out.

Max used the rail ticket to travel to Genoa, the refunded remainder then available for immediate lodging and meals. Soon, with the last of the liras running out, Max directed his next appeal to the *Judische Cultursgemeinde*, a Jewish cultural association, where he was the recipient of immediate assistance and counsel. Board and lodging were arranged for him. He now gave up any hope of going to America—for the present. In Genoa, at the Cultursgemeinde Max requested and was given, a note to the French consulate. He would attempt his alternative plan which was to go to France where he had the chance to utilize a family attachment: namely, Helena Rubinstein, another cousin to his mother, a woman in the business of cosmetics and beauty aids. Max mentioned no one by name; he left details ambiguous, fearing the secretary at the consulate might contact Mme. Rubinstein and that he could encounter her rejection before he had a chance for a vis-a-vis to employ his already well-developed charm and capacity for manipulation. The consul issued Max a student visa to France; the boy then returned to the Cultursgemeinde to say he would need money for the fare. He assured repayment and he was given a rail ticket to Marseilles, although his objective was to reach Paris.

It was only then that he wrote to his parents of his proposed plan and destination. Now, for the first time the German speaking boy was confronted with a language problem, for he knew not a word of French and all around him in Marseilles—this busy seaport to which he arrived—he heard this strange, incomprehensible tongue. Friendless, hampered by an inability to speak the country's language, without money--it was imperative that he find fellow-Jews. Most spoke and understand at least a little of the Yiddish language, he reasoned. But in Marseilles the Jews were almost exclusively *Sephardim*, ethnically Spanish Jews whose folk language was *Ladino*, a Spanish derived dialect, whereas Yiddish was a corrupted Germanic language that was spoken by Jews of Eastern and Central Europe. Fortunately among these Ladino-speaking Jews some did know Yiddish because of business contacts, and Max was optimistic that he would

55

find someone with whom he could communicate to convey his need of help in getting to Paris. It was at the railway station that Max made the acquaintance of Isaac Rosenfeld, a Russian Jew living in France. Isaac had come to Marseilles to escort his wife and daughter to a ship sailing to Palestine. Mrs. Rosenfeld, a Palestine Jewess, was on her way to visit her family. Rosenfeld was returning home to Paris when Max engaged him in conversation at the station. Although an *Ashkenazim*, one of the Jews having knowledge of Yiddish, Isaac Rosenfeld did not. And he had only a very slight understanding of German; but communication was not impossible.

This man who himself had been a refugee not too many years before, instinctively understood the plight of the boy. He fell in with Max's scheme to repeat his previous success by concealment while a controller passed through the train checking tickets. This time he at least had a passport and a visa and was already within the confines of France with the legal right to be there. The precariousness of his situation was minimal. As was done to implement the subterfuge in Poland, acquaintances of his new-found benefactor joined Mr. Rosenfeld and Max in their compartment. The trouser legs of the men shielded the illicit rider crouched beneath the banquette. Salami, bread, and bottled water were offered by the men. Max accepted gratefully. "But who are these family members who will take you in charge?" one of the men queried Max. "There is a woman who has a business, a cousin of my mother's. Her name is Helena Rubinstein and I think she will be able to help me." The men burst into laughter, prodding each other and winking knowingly. "You will be all right, my boy," said Max's patron, "I can see you have nothing to worry about." Far better than Max these men knew of the success and wealth of the "woman who has a business."

Upon arrival at Gare de Lyon, one of the principal railway stations in Paris, one of the four men left the train, turning in his ticket to the collector at the gate. Then he went to a machine which dispenses visitors' tickets: *les tiquets de quay*, costing a few centimes. He purchased two such tickets, one to enable him to return to the train as if meeting a passenger, and one for Max so that he too could pass through the gate as though he had just gone to meet the train and was now leaving.

Rosenfeld took Max to his home and to a comfortable bed. The boy was dirty, unkempt and exhausted from spending the night on the floor of the train, beneath the seats, as well as from the tension, excitement. The following noon the two went to a cafe where Max began to make the acquaintance of several other Jewish immigrants among the people congregated there during the busy lunch hours. Rosenfeld telephoned the office of Helena Rubinstein to announce that a young fellow from Poland had come to Paris and was seeking members of his family. Mme. Rubinstein was out of the country on a business trip. She was not expected to be back for several months. It was her nephew, Oscar Kolin who came to pick up Max and arrange his care and tutelage for the interval until Helena herself returned to make decisions others were not authorized to make.

Oscar Kolin and Max conversed in German. Max explained the family relationship and told Oscar he had come to live in France, but didn't do more than gloss over the details of how he had arrived to the country. The image of a rebellious runaway was not a prudent one to portray, the boy was wise enough to realize. It was to Mr. and Mrs. Hirschberg, Mme. Rubinstein's sister and brother-in-law that Max was taken when he and Oscar left the home of Rosenfeld. Oscar thanked the host warmly and politely, expressing gratitude for the help and protection he had given to one of their family members. Pauline Rubinstein Hirschberg was the second born of the eight Rubinstein daughters, Helena being the eldest. Pauline was a cheerful, understanding woman who handled with tact the hostile, bitter personality of her husband. Hirschberg had suffered such a severe blow to his head as a boy that his head leaned almost to one shoulder. The afflicted boy forever hated the father who had thus struck him, and he projected his anger upon all who had dealings with him. To add to his unhappy fate came the realization that he was to remain childless.

Mme. Hirschberg was patient and gentle. She continually made allowances and rationalizations for her husband's bad temper. Perhaps she found sufficient fulfillment in her career at the Helena Rubinstein Institute, for she held an important position, one that kept her very busy. Mr. Hirschberg was a success in his own business of the manufacturing of fur coats.

When Oscar Kolin brought Max to the home of the Hirschbergs, an open discussion ensued. Upon mutual agreement Pauline and her husband would keep the boy in their home. Until Helena came back Max could not be invited to take a job or enter a training program in the Helena Rubinstein Institute, although Mr. Kolin and Mrs. Hirschberg agreed it was very likely that "the Madame." would be delighted to have a bright young family member added to her staff. But until that was a certainty Mr. Hirschberg suggested that Max report every day to his factory where he would begin to learn the detailed and precise functions of cutting animal skins for fur garments. The trade was principally in minks. Even as raw skins, these were very expensive. Max was not allowed to do his beginning apprenticeship on such costly materials. Instead he was to learn to wield the sharp scalpel-like furrier's knife on the hides of rabbits. As the steel blade bit into the pelts their fine silky hairs drifted into the air. These pesky intruders offended Max's nose and throat, drawn in as he breathed over his work. His hands grew painful from cuts and bruises occasioned by hours of gripping the knife. His muscles screamed in outrage at remaining immobile as he stood for hours bent over his task at the cutting table. Mr. Hirschberg was harsh and demanding. Man and boy clashed repeatedly until one day Hirschberg struck Max. Angrily the boy shouted: "If you ever do that again I shall show how I can straighten up your head for you." After that Max told Mrs. Hirschberg that he would no longer work in her husband's factory and that it would be better if he left their home. A room and board arrangement was made for him with a family known to be suitably respectable and responsible.

Returning often to the cafes that were frequented particularly by the many Jewish immigrants from central and eastern Europe, Max soon met Israel Hasenpouth, a well-educated, highly intelligent and politically sophisticated Russian immigrant. Mr. Hasenpouth, too, was a successful furrier, but an ardent socialist as well. His liking for Max was immediate and deep. After one or two meetings Israel said he wanted Max to meet his son Jacques who was the same age as Max. Jacques was in a trade school for apprenticeship in fur manufacturing. It was a boarding school and the young fellow came home only on weekends. As soon as they were brought together through Jacques' father the two boys became inseparable companions. Where you saw Max you saw Jacques, and whenever you encountered Jacques you were bound to find Max. Partly through this Parisian born friend Max swiftly assimilated into the cultural milieu of French youth, picking up the language, the tastes, the point of view and the general life-style of young people in urban France during those wine-and-roses years of the Twenties.

When "the Madame," Helena Rubinstein returned to Paris she and Max had their first meeting. She conversed with him in German, in Polish, in Yiddish. "The first thing we must do," the lady executive directed, "is to send you to a school that will teach you quickly and correctly to speak the French language." In a few months Max was speaking with remarkable fluency. He had a talent for languages and an enthusiasm for this new one.

The Helena Rubinstein Institute and Laboratory, where all the formulas were developed and tested was in St. Cloud, outside Paris. Max was assigned to work and study at the Institute; at first he was required to live there, coming to Paris only on week-ends.

Although in private Max was to call Helena and also her sister Pauline "auntie," he was careful to use the formal appellations of "Mme. Rubinstein" and "Mme. Hirschberg" when he encountered them at the Institute, in the presence of employees not related to the family. Even so, as soon as it was known that Max Neuman was part of the Rubinstein clan there were uncomfortable manifestations of jealousy. The director became a subtly more demanding taskmaster; he and the other upper-level employees felt insecure and even paranoid, believing Max was spying on them, reporting infractions to "the Madame" and being groomed as a replacement for one of them.

When Max was about sixteen and was sufficiently trained in the basics of cosmetology, his patroness said it was time for the serious and arduous training in the chemistry and experimentations of cosmetics formulae. Max would have to make the decision to devote the next six years to intensive tutelage and study, abandoning frivolities he now reveled in on the week-ends and evenings. More and more week-ends of self-indulgence were resulting in failure to show up at the Institute on Mondays. He had already given up residence in St. Cloud, accepted the invitation to live at the home of the Hasenpouths, occupying Jacques' room during the week and sharing it with Jacques on the week-ends.

The outline of the program described to Max by Madame Rubinstein discouraged him. It sounded rigid, dismal and of appalling discipline. To his later regret Max declined; he held only a non-significant place in the Institute. But until the close of the Second World War he had the generous patronage of "Auntie Helene." During the war, when he was in London in 1943, 1944 and 1945 he could still find funds available to supplement his military pay at the branch of the company there.

While at the Institute—and even after—Helena Rubinstein supported Max in the financial "playboy" style that nourished his self-indulgence; she mistakenly believed he would outgrow his irresponsibility to eventually take a proper place in the business. He never did, and in 1936 lost the opportunity she retained for him until he flouted her authority and approval by joining the International Brigade that went to Spain to support the Republican cause in the Spanish Civil War.

Mme. Rubinstein was mystified and distressed by the strength of Max's anti-fascist convictions which she believed might have a suspicious tinge of pro-socialism. Although generous and philanthropic, the wealthy and successful woman held aristocratic conceptions, even aspiring to marry deposed royalty, thus obtaining the title of "Princess Gourelli" in 1938. She married Prince Artchie Gourelli-Tchkonia of Georgia (U.S.S.R.) the same year of her divorce to Edward J. Titus, her first husband, and father to her two sons. Max retained a fondness and respect for Titus; he disliked "the Prince" and made no effort to conceal it, responding often in "biting and baiting" tones to conversation initiated by Gourelli.

Max's parents as well, although simple, religious folk were "landed gentry" for generations. They, too, were steeped in

Jewish aristocratic sentiments, but based upon the snobbism of "the most pious" and "the most scholarly," rather than upon wealth. Nowhere in the family would he find any support for the kind of "get in there and fight for the oppressed" that Max had been exposed to since mingling with the Parisian liberals and intellectuals who gathered in popular cafes of the city. Indeed, he was a bundle of paradoxes, for he kept a foot in each of two conflicting philosophies: the rational intellectualism of the educated working class and students, and the parasitic mentality of the idle rich, not only French but also of the other nationals that made of Paris a wonderful international playground.

Max's years from 1927 to 1939 comprised a period of intense development, made possible by the total lack of constraints. He was free of parental restriction while living in Paris at a time of optimal opportunities for the acquisition of cultural understandings in fields of literature, music, theater, painting and sculpture. It was an era of political enlightenment and consciousness raising, of free dialogue and critical examination, an atmosphere of acceptance of change and of challenge. There was for Max an enthralling release from the excruciating bonds that he had writhed under and flailed against in his early years. Now he tore and ripped and flung them off, all but self-immolating in the excesses of freedom.

Several of the most outstanding modern American writers were living in Paris during this period. Many of their works were published by Edward Titus, the first husband of Helena Rubinstein. Mr. Titus showed his liking for Max in various ways, one of which was to invite him to be a privileged "auditor" at the round table forum at the Cafe du Dome, a notable coffee house and meeting place in the heart of the city. There Titus and a few literary figures whom Titus described as *"la creme du monde literaire"* gathered to engage in

62

dialogue and repartee and frequently animated disagreement on a variety of controversial issues. Protocol demanded that Max refrain from active participation, but the experience of merely being present to hear and observe these already—or soon-to-be famous writers was as valuable to Max's education and developing sophistication as would have been a series of courses at the Sorbonne.

It was through Edward Titus that Max became a close friend of Horace Titus, the younger son of Titus and of Helena Rubinstein. Through this association Max learned many of the refinements of upper class French life styles. He cultivated his tastes for elegant food and wines, he frequented and learned to appreciate, to understand classical ballet, the symphony, the opera. He read classical French literature, as well as popular modern novels. Max followed Horace's recommendations in his choice of a tailor and boot maker. He occupied, rent free, an apartment in the fashionable neighborhood of Faubourg-St. Honore, in a building owned by Helena Rubinstein. At young people's dances Max learned the "in" steps and routines, and he enjoyed night spots featuring the ribald "Can-Can" and dances of "the Apaches," the lively, happy club life of diversion that appealed to a high-spirited carefree young fellow coming to the end of his teen years and beginning of his twenties.

Young, handsome, well-tailored, well-funded, and now with an acquired polish that differed markedly from the accepted manner of upper-class orthodox Jews in small central European cities, Max Neuman found life utterly enchanting!

Ever sports-minded Max continued to love skiing and skating, the winter activities he learned almost before he was more than a toddler. To these diversions he soon added other skills: tennis and horseback riding. Horace Titus introduced him to polo and hurdle horse jumping. Although he practiced well enough to become good at the latter, Max never mastered well enough—nor liked—polo. He went along on hunting expeditions which included the high risks of shooting wild boar. As he recollected: "You'd better not miss killing the boar, for he is an indomitable foe!" The danger was thrilling and exhilarating.

Max was a member of the Touring Club of France, often joining the groups for camping trips and mountain climbing. He owned a motorcycle, learned to race it. As soon as he was eligible for a license to drive a car, he did so, and bought one of his own.

The great books Max read of the history of France were the fiery, stirring writings of Voltaire, of Rousseau, of Zola. He read books and papers on Zionism, growing feverish with the dream. Influenced and inspired by conversations with Jacques' father and other proponents of the socialist creed and program for world economic and political ethics, Max read Karl Marx and Friedrich Engels. He was intensely committed to the Socialist-Zionist vision of a Jewish homeland in Palestine.

Intermittently, when not too busy with the priorities of his social life Max reported to the Institute for his work and duties. He made a point of being in attendance with greater regularity when "the Madame" was in Paris, for then her watchful eye upon him served as a reminder that she was the source of all these wondrous benefits, and only possible through her generous allowance. Money came from home as well, but hardly would have proved sufficient for the lifestyle Max enjoyed until the commencement of the Second World War.

Although Mme. Rubinstein did not go so far as to curtail her financial support, from time to time Max's connection with the company was interrupted and later with the Madame herself. During those interludes he took jobs which gave him independent work experience and further augmented his supply of money. But even after the final clash between Max and Helena Rubinstein when there ensued an angry confrontation over the young man's resolve to go to Spain to support that country's anti-fascist cause against Francisco Franco, the money was not cut off. Even during the Second World War years Max regularly found a substantial stipend allocated to him at the London branch of the company.

By 1938 Max regretted his arrogant and flagrant disregard of his patroness' demands. His connection to the company and the influential name of Helena Rubinstein would have enabled him to go to London or New York. Instead he had to endure perilous years as a fugitive, a Resistance fighter, incarceration in Spain after his escape from France, and ultimately an air combatant with the active Free French Forces attached to the British Royal Air Force. Following the war's end his service was demanded as a translator at the war crimes trials in Nuremberg and to help in the de-Nazification work for the United Nations Relief and Rehabilitation Agency (U.N.R.R.A.) in occupied Germany.

A period of eight years was encompassed during the prime of Max's life.

"Pondering the 1925 to 1939 era I have a sense of having dreamed or fantasized the joy, the freedom, the unrestrained self-indulgence and self-expression of that period of my life. I had emerged from a shadowy cove to bask in glistening warm sunlight for a brief time. But then I found myself plunged into darkness so profound that I can never recover my vision sufficiently to see clearly the beauty once so apparent and so available. My youthful confidence in my ability to control my destiny was forever eroded by the sobering reality of my vulnerability and the limitations of my power to even survive, let alone envelope myself in a cocoon of softness and sweetness."

Apart from books and cafe table discussions, Max's

political consciousness-raising developed through his active participation in youth groups that concerned themselves intensively with Zionism. He attended lectures, debates and a series of campaigns to combat racism and anti-Semitism. The latter doctrine was incorporated into *La Ligue Contre le Fascisme et l'Anti-Semitisme.*

A Zionist right wing organization of which Max was a member was the *Brith Trumfelder*, known by the acronym BETAR and headed by Vladimir Jabotinski. It was an ultra-nationalistic para-military group, brown shirted, leather belted, which when called to assemble at demonstrations armed its members with brickbats.

One of the significant confrontations between the BETAR and an organization of fascist youths occurred as early as 1931 during the showing of the play, *L'Affaire Dreyfus* which was protested by *L'Action Francaise* and other fascist anti-Semitic groups. Crowds of their members gathered to sabotage the play by marching in front of the theater, shouting and attempting in every way to impede or embarrass would-be theater-goers. They threw stench bombs, created great disturbance and even made some assaults on patrons attempting to enter the theater, The BETAR along with members of other Jewish youth groups appeared on the scene to counter the attacks. The fascist youths attached razors to their brickbats, the Jews followed suit. Countless non-Jewish sympathizers arrived to help the Jewish cause and the police met the overwhelming pro-Jewish resistance with only token attempts to deter them. The fascists fell back and scattered in disarray.

After the terrifying *Kristallnacht* in Germany in 1938, when every synagogue and other Jewish institutions and facilities were raided, desecrated, smashed, destroyed throughout Germany, and as reports of other disturbances of this terrifying, dastardly nature reached France there was greater frequency to the meetings of young Jews, each item of news prompting heightened anti-fascist activity. Beginning with the time of the completion of his national military conscription in 1934 Max became a political activist in the full sense of the term.

These activities were met with more than moderate annoyance and disapproval from patroness Helena Rubinstein. She found Max's participation an embarrassment. In addition such interests were keeping him from his duties at the Institute, and evoking murmurs and comments from non-familial employees who resented the laxity Max was permitted. Mme. Hirschberg was one of the most indulgent of the senior staff members, but careful not to let Mme. Rubinstein know how much she was covering up for the young man and how often she was adding a bit of her own money to his already outrageously fat purse! The childless "Auntie Pauline" had a special weakness for the intense lad who fired up the atmosphere and radiated so much energy that even his curly hair seemed to be charged with vigor and purpose.

Max won female hearts easily, young hearts and older hearts, for he cut a dashing figure. He did not just move, he bounded vibrantly. Although very temperate in his drinking he smoked excessively; always a cigarette dangled from a shapely mouth above which a thin well-barbered moustache was cultivated. How well he knew his attributes and how shamelessly he exploited them! They proved to be his trump card but also his undoing, for he learned to rely too heavily upon the power of charisma. Time after time he missed significant opportunities for real self-development and lasting skills. Those who let him win this way instead of earning his way were, in the end, his real betrayers. Perennially he employed his methods of manipulating his milieu rather than triumphing through superiority and excellence. His rebellious disregard for discipline and his life-long lack of *self*-discipline except—fortunately—when his very survival was at stake, resulted in a resistance to any academic demands that required patience and hard work: if it didn't come easily it was abandoned.

Paradoxically he thrived on challenges of personality. The more difficult it was to gain control of a situation by means of verbal exchange, and even by intimidation which his strong well-developed body made credible, the more determined he was to emerge triumphant. As a young child he concluded that to be cunning, to be strong and to be swift was to avert pain at the hands of the nasty little gentile boys—*the goyim*—who plagued and terrified the timid, passive Jewish schoolboys whose only recourse seemed to be flight from the taunting bullies who pursued them for the sheer sport of tearing at their curling ear locks, trampling hats and books, and often bloodying their sniffling noses. In short order word got around: "Stay away from Max Neuman; he can lick you." Many a beaten-up boy, particularly one whose shirt had been ripped to shreds gave solemn testimony of the fearless, ferocious Jewish kid who stood his ground against Polish fists and cries of "Christ killer."

Even as a youngster complexities in Max emerged that puzzled others. In diametric opposition to the arrogance, aggressiveness and self-eccentricity, aspects of protectiveness, gentleness and even sympathetic patience characterized aspects of his behavior while still very young. In Lizensk when Max was a little boy there was a cerebral palsied child, ridiculed, disdained and isolated. Often Max would seek him out at the boy's home, sit and talk and play simple quiet games within the capacity of this child with handicaps and limitations. The boy who was so downcast brightened and livened in Max's presence. The other boys were curious and mystified. "Why do you bother about that useless idiot?" they wanted to know, not comprehending the satisfaction Max felt. The eager, grateful expressions were very rewarding to Max when he appeared for an hour's play, providing the only friendship among the town's children.

Many causes and many people were championed in the course of Max's life because of what he perceived to be their vulnerability to the tides that sweep mercilessly over the weak and helpless. No one can say what is an act of altruism and what is the raw material of egoism, but there is a strong suggestion that in the nature of the truly strong there is a sense of responsibility that motivates them to behave as "rescuers." It is interesting to note here that Max's first two wives were on the brink of motherhood when their hasty trips to the altar with him averted the awkwardness of single parenthood. His third wife, your author, was a divorcee in marginally adequate health with a frail little girl—the two living alone at a great distance from their family—when Max came into their lives. Indeed, other factors attracted him but from time to time, during the marriage, Max would like to conjecture upon how they would have ever have gotten by without him! At times it appeared he was quite right.

Chapter Five
My Dichotomy

In 1932 Max was confronted with the inevitability of required military service. A letter from Mme. Rubinstein stating he had just begun an intensive course of study in chemistry won him a two year deferment. After the first year, 1933, Max decided it was just as well to get the conscription period behind him. He reported for service, saying he was terminating his studies. At age 21 he reluctantly accepted this pause in "la vie en rose." *Au revoir* to the club life: social, sporting, and political. Also to the delights of the *Comedie Francaise* and the classical and modern dramas of the French theater. Farewell—for the time being—to leisurely hours of reading light and heavy literature that included not only the great writers of France but of Russia, Germany, and other cultures as well. These sources had broadened and deepened his learning, particularly in geography, history, and political science.

The upwardly mobile side of him enjoyed the pretensions of appearing at the opera and the symphony in full evening dress, complete in winter with top hat and opera cape! These evenings of attendance at the opera were more a matter of adopting status symbols; he often felt restless and bored, looking forward to their conclusion so he and his "date" could move on to supper at a fashionable night spot and a few hours of dancing in some racy *cave*, as the basement-level small clubs were called.

After reporting for recruitment Max was scheduled for the

physical examination, along with other prospective inductees. This procedure was public but mostly attended by ladies past their youth who watch from the gallery. They gaze down upon the scene of a series of doctors, each of whom is busy with the testing of another portion of the nude men. As each man completes the medical check-up, he is evaluated; and, if found to be in good physical condition, he is told to report for induction. When he is dressed, a group of these spectator ladies, as a committee, present him with the badge of pride which reads: *Bon Pour Le Service*, Fit For Service. Until the man is in uniform he wears this symbol of commendation; everywhere he is congratulated and made to feel he is the height of nobility and valor.

Before the induction Max's friends took him out for the evening, a traditional event similar to the bridegroom's bachelor party on the eve of his wedding. It turned out to be an integral part of his growing up process, for it was his enlightenment on homosexuality. The group went to a cafe where transvestites and transsexuals were the performers; the entire concept had been unknown to Max before this. After performing a song and dance number, filled with coquetry, sexual innuendos and suggestive lyrics and movements, one of the attractive performers came to the table of Max and his companions to pay homage to the new military recruit. "She" sat down next to the guest of honor and led on his eager advances. Soon his hand found its way to "her" crotch and his sex lesson came in a flash, amid gales of laughter from the other fellows as his face grew crimson with embarrassment. He only then realized that not all coupling is between a man and a woman and that his friends had contrived to teach him this fact in this manner, before sending him off to the army.

Before going away, Max sold his well-equipped motorcycle and his Citroen sports car, locked up his plush bachelor apartment on Av. Faubourg-St. Honore, and bade au revoir, chivalrously but without any special sense of loss for Odette Gabe, his seventeen year old girl friend. He began to look forward to the next year-and-a-half as a new adventure.

The routine of induction was not unlike that of other Western countries: another series of examinations, tests to assess intelligence, personality, skills and interests; there were varied means of judging aptitudes. Then the inductees were interviewed for the purpose of making a final decision on the branch of service to which the man would be assigned. It was rumored that the military appeared to take some perverse delight in asking a man where he would prefer to serve and then assigning him to a branch quite unlike his choice. Max, well-prepared for such battles of wits earnestly declared that he had chosen the infantry on the questionnaire that related to preferences because it seemed the most "rugged and soldierly" of all branches. The interviewing officer smiled slyly to the associate seated beside him at the long desk between them and Max. "This man seems to be best suited for attachment to infantry." The assisting clerk filled in the assignment form. And that is how Max went into the air corps, the branch he so fervently sought!

Strenuous training began and Max's athletic prowess became apparent to his drill sergeant. He was singled out and groomed for all the sports competitions within his regiment, between regiments and among the various branches of the service in the region, and finally throughout France. Time after time he brought victory and honor to whomever he represented. He was offered the chance to train as one of his country's athletes in Olympic games. He would have to agree to remain in the service for five years, a condition that was unacceptable to Max. He did, though, excel in track meets, including hurdle jumping. Too, he engaged in boxing matches until numerous punches to his nose made him decline to take further risks in the ring after his nose was broken. A disfigured face was more than he was willing to accept to achieve glory, or contrarily, perhaps to end up quite ingloriously.

*   *   *

Max's relationship with Odette Gabe had been both intimate and long-standing. She was his mistress for two years without the consequence of parenthood for the young couple; but then the *accident* occurred. Before Max's induction he was presented with the news of impending fatherhood. The situation was discussed with Odette's parents—her mother, and her step-father, Marcel Gasse. Gasse was liberal in his ideas and neutral on the matter of a pragmatic marriage. Odette's mother was the designated negotiator, assuring Max that all that was expected of him was the granting of temporary legal status to her pregnant daughter, with no further responsibility for the child. Max was disturbed by this turn of events which did not fit into his plans to have a few more years of the freedom of bachelorhood before settling into a serious career and family responsibilities. That immediate emotional response gave way to deeper soul searching. It required him to confront the fact that marriage to a non-Jewish girl was not ever his intention. The only commitment he then made to Odette and her family was to give the matter consideration. He rationalized that it was incumbent upon the female to protect the relationship from such unwanted intruders, which he considered a baby to be. He might, but on the other hand, he might not commit the "charitable" act of marrying this girl who had been remiss in her duty. Assuredly, if they did marry it would be viewed by Max as a "rescue" rather than a matter of sharing the mutual responsibilities of their love-making.

The correspondence between Odette and Max was infrequent and rather casual, but in her letters the mother-to-be repeated the suggestion that being born of

74

married parents would give the child the respectability to which it was entitled. And that it was important to her own status, as well. Fortuitously, a new military directive was instrumental in tipping the scale in Odette's favor. There was an attempt to mitigate the hardship of separation between servicemen and their wives and children. For Max it would mean that if he became a family man he would have the opportunity to be transferred from the air base at which he was stationed, in a remote rural area to a post just outside of Paris. Intriguing prospect! He was agonizingly bored, and extremely eager to be able to spend leaves and week-end passes in a livelier and more exciting manner.

The commanding officer of Max's post was General Jacob Leon Weiller, a Jewish hero of the First World War. As an activist in liberal causes, he and Max had an apparent rapport. Although the general was a native born Frenchman, Max believed that he would understand Max's reticence and doubts about contemplating marriage to a Gentile. The young recruit went to see the general to obtain advice on this perplexing subject. What he really hoped for from General Weiller was reinforcement of his profound unwillingness to effect this alliance. The discussion between the two men included an outline of Max's family background. His history included many well-known and honored rabbis. The strict orthodoxy to which his parents adhered could find absolutely no acceptance of this contemplated union. But as the time was approaching for his child to be born, Max was stricken with his usual impulse to protect the vulnerable. Always slothful about resolving knotty conflicts he took the coward's way out and tossed the weight of the decision into the hands of this father figure, his commanding officer. He expressed one last thread of protest and resistance, however, saying: "I always kept in mind that when I found myself ready for marriage I would return to the city of my parents and there look for a young girl I could love, who would also be suitable to our family." It was almost spoken in reverie, for clearly the commanding officer was focused on his own convictions on the subject.

Gen. Weiller summed it up thus: "Young man, if the girl was good enough to be your mistress, she is good enough to be your wife!" The post script he added was, "I am giving you a weeks's leave to go to Paris. Let me know if you have married and if so your transfer to Paris will be effected immediately." Not long after, Max learned that the wife of Gen. Weiller was a French woman and a Gentile, and so there had been no real chance of an unbiased attitude. Max communicated his decision to Odette and the arrangements got underway for the nuptials to take place.

At the *mairie*, the city hall, the guests in attendance at the brief ceremony were Odette's mother, Marcel Gasse, Odette's sister and brother, Max's closest friend Jacques Hasenpouth, and a young woman named Josette. Josette was the girl friend of both Jacques and Max on a "shared" basis. That is, there were designated days when she was Max's girl, and some on which she "belonged" to Jacques. Often all three went out together, but Josette and the two men came to this mutually acceptable arrangement because the two friends were in love with Josette and Josette was in love with the two friends! She was captivated by the aesthetic, poetic, gentle personality of Jacques; she was enchanted by Max's skill as a dancer, his stimulating energy, and his roguish ways.

Odette and Max held hands across the enormous bulge of the bride's middle occasioned by her advanced stage of pregnancy, and they recited the vows. When it was over the bride, the groom, and the guests went to the wedding reception Marcel Gasse hosted. The elaborate luncheon meal was an almost all afternoon event. It took place in a fine restaurant where one of the private rooms was reserved for the party. Then Odette went home with her parents to await the birth of her child. Max re-opened his apartment now that he was able to be in Paris again, and spent the wedding night there, alone. A most unusual way to begin marriage, to be sure. Three days later the bride and groom became parents. A son was born to them; he was named Claude Denis Camille Neuman, soon after baptized in the Catholic Church. As far as Max was concerned he had fulfilled a duty, for now the boy need not suffer the stigma attached to those whose birth certificates and other official documents bore the words: _pere inconnu_, father unknown. But in other ways the child's life would be untraditional; at a very young age Claude was sent away to the country to be raised by his great grandmother, Odette's grandmother.

The birth occurred just before Max's leave expired. He telephoned to the air corps base to request additional leave, which was invariably granted for such events as new fatherhood. Max asked to be connected with the office of Gen. Weiller and to speak to the general himself." _Mazel Tov_," "Good Luck," the general shouted into the phone. "As soon as your extended leave expires come back to the base to pack your gear. Your transfer is in process, and you will have the chance to be close to your wife and your son!"

It was August 1933; Max had been in the air corps five months. The next 13 months of service became considerably sweeter now that every free hour of the day could be spent in Paris. Max was no longer at an air corps base. He was assigned to an administerial office in the city. His duties were as untaxing and uncomplicated as one could imagine. They consisted of approving requisitions for high octane gasoline for use in planes. Allocations were issued based upon a given formula. All Max had to do was to determine the proper allotment and pass the forms to a ranking officer for signature. Free by 5 p.m. each day, and on week-ends, he was more liberated from duties than any working civilian might be. Even wearing a uniform when off duty was not a requirement. One day, however, while attending a Yom Kippur, Day of Atonement service at the largest and most prestigious synagogue in Paris, "La Synagogue Rothschild," Max met Gen. Weiller again. They greeted each other with the usual *Bonne Annee,* "Happy New Year," and the general commended Max for being at the temple in uniform. Max was glad that in this small way he had done something gratifying to this man who had gone out of his way to arrange a military position that only could be obtained through important influence.

Not only could the serviceman live in his own apartment, he was also granted a housing allowance. For Odette and Claude there was a dependency allowance, which Max put to use for himself. Although the money orders were in his wife's name they were addressed to him. Odette, as the wife of a serviceman and the mother of his child, but additionally the orphaned daughter of a deceased First World War veteran, had the choice of living in a military compound. There was one in Nancy, 600 kms. from Paris. Her grandmother lived in Toul, 24 kms. from Nancy. Odette decided it would be a happy, healthful place for her baby to start life. She and Claude shared one of the bungalows in the compound with another young serviceman's family, a mother with one small child. For all these wives and their children there was a diverting program of social and sports activities. It was a satisfactory situation for this new nuclear family of Neumans, particularly for Max. He was unencumbered by the marriage, and even had the audacity to use the family allowance for himself. He induced Odette's sister to meet him each month after the arrival of the money order. She would present *le Livret de Mariage,* the "Marriage Booklet" to the postal clerk who would then cash the money order. Jeanette, neither bright nor with any sisterly loyalty was a willing accomplice in return for a pleasant lunch to which Max treated her after she cashed the voucher and gave him the money.

A servicemen's philanthropic organization also supplemented Max's income from time to time. It was a voluntary group working with donations to be used to subsidize the needs of servicemen. They provided varying amounts of cash to Max, which he asked for on the pretext of needing to meet expenses to visit his wife and child in Nancy and to bring items of clothing for his rapidly growing young son.

From time to time Max moved up in rank to that of a sergeant but not to be retained long! With the rank came the requirement to be on duty certain weekends, and often later in the day. Max would find a way to be "broken." This happened a few times and finally, on one occasion after an infraction was committed and his rank was again reduced to corporal, his superior officer was livid with pique. "One more time, Neuman, and you shall face a court ✿martial." It was merely two months before he was to be discharged and Max knew the threat was idle. Much later he learned that serving his two years as a conscript followed by the war years from 1939 to 1946 he would have had considerably greater retirement benefits by having maintained a higher rank. In April 1934 Max was discharged as a reservist. Mme. Max Neuman, nee Odette Valentine Marie Helene Gabe was now expected to fulfill her part of the "bargain" which included divorcing Max when he left the air corps. She began to manifest reluctance, finding the state of marriage not distasteful even with an absent husband. Odette delayed the filing of a petition for divorce, although Max pressed the issue and reminded her of her promise. "Well, then you apply for it," she retorted. "It would not be nice for me to brand you as an adulteress," Max argued. "I am well-known to have been an unfaithful husband, and for you to bring charges would be more seemly and more credible."

They came to terms, sharing equally the legal cost; Odette charged her husband with adultery, the only grounds for divorce in France at that time. But the hindrance of a three-year wait until the issuance of a final decree could not be circumvented. It was only in 1937 that Max was finally free of this sham marriage. Odette assumed her maiden name and went on with life as a single woman, but now with a child she did not wish to raise. She never remarried.

Max did little for their son. However, in 1936 before leaving to fight in Spain during that country's civil war he assigned any posthumous benefits that might accrue, to Claude. Also in 1939 when he was mobilized at the start of the Second World War he removed his savings from the bank and gave them to Odette for the boy. Max had no other part in his son's upbringing other than to answer Odette's request for his help when their son needed a father's counsel after getting into adolescent scrapes a few times. Nevertheless, Claude grew to manhood, served in the Algerian encounter with the French army, learned the skills of a plumber and became a stable husband and a father of two girls. He became a middle-class skilled tradesman, tall, dark, and Gaullist in appearance, but unremarkable although he did indicate high intelligence as a youngster and as a teenager. His parents gave him little more than the avoidance of embarrassment of being Claude Denis Gabe, *pere inconnu*. Later, tiring of the arduous tasks of plumbing he took the requisite training and started to work as a bank clerk.

One of the benefits to Max—through his connection with Odette's family—was a long-term friendship with Marcel Gasse, the artistically-talented and fascinating step-father of Odette. Gasse was a de-facto husband, a partner in what the French call *un mariage derriere l'eglise*, a marriage "behind" the church. Gasse and Odette's mother forged their alliance not long after the woman became a war widow. She and her three orphaned children were the recipients of a substantial pension after Monsieur Gabe was killed in action during the First World War. The benefits would have evaporated if the widow remarried; the absence of this technicality in no way detracted from the loyalty and devotion of the de-facto spouses who remained lifelong partners. Marcel Gasse sculpted and fashioned fine, aged woods into the highest quality and most beautiful furniture to be found in Paris. He perfected each piece: choosing the timber carefully, treating it, shaping and carving, joining and finishing it with the utmost care, skill, and pride. Gasse had great affection for Max. The young man and his father-in-law engaged in dialogues on politics and philosophy. Marcel remained a loyal friend and benefactor during the bad times after the collapse of France, sheltering Max at times, and keeping some of his possessions for him when Max became a fugitive at the commencement of the Nazi occupation. Despite the war years that separated Max from many of his friends, the two men resumed the friendship when Max returned to France after the liberation

After his eighteenth-month hitch in the military, when Max returned to civilian life, he stepped up his pro-Zionist and anti-fascist activities. He also volunteered to work with a Jewish boy scout troop as their leader. And he joined _The Maccabees_, a Jewish sport and cultural association of young men and women who met for competitions in athletic games. They had started, in 1932, to hold international sports meets which were known as the "Jewish Olympics." Max's sports training in the air force equipped him to become a successful candidate for the 1935 Maccabi games, and to lead the French delegation bound for the competitions in Palestine that year. The group traveled from Paris to Vienna to join other young people. These were German-speaking who felt

81

more comfortable among their French counterparts because of Max, bi-lingual "bridge" between the two language groups.

When the games were over, Max stayed in Palestine for a period that lasted six months. A footloose bachelor again, now that his divorce was in process, and with money to ensure the pleasures of travel, Max enjoyed beaches, parties and dances with the young men and women he met there. A very pretty and popular girl named Mella fell under the Frenchman's charm. A departing diplomat sold him, cheaply, an outrageously ostentatious Packard car and Max drove Mella everywhere in it. He even bought her an engagement ring as a symbol of his affection and serious intentions. Mella's wealthy parents, born in Palestine of European descendants, owned a large first-class hotel. They thoroughly approved of their daughter's choice and were prepared to share their business interests with her prospective husband so that he could provide suitably for Mella.

Max came out of the spell abruptly, and departed hastily when he realized that he had grown to adore the splendor of Parisian life too much to abandon it. He left a heart-broken girl and her angry, indignant family. He also left the Packard. It was not easily saleable because of its greedy consumption of fuel. He parked it at a curbside and walked away from it the day he was leaving to go back to France.

Decades later, on a summer evening in 1961, at a sidewalk cafe in Haifa, Max and Mella saw one another for the first time since 1935. Max and Shirley Ann—his third wife—were on a lengthy tour of Europe with a side trip to Israel. All at once the manager of this Israeli cafe announced the closing of his establishment as the eve of a holiday of fasting was approaching. It was *Tisha b'Av*, the ninth day of the Hebrew month of Av, which is a day of mourning in the Jewish religion, memorializing the anniversary of the fall of both the First and the Second Temples of bible history.

Max, Shirley and another couple had been chatting while enjoying refreshments, and rose to leave when they were finished. From the next table came a woman's voice saying: "Max, Max Neuman!" Hearing his name, Max turned and saw a stout woman smiling and beckoning to him. He did not recognize her. "I see you do not recall," she continued, "I am Mella R; we knew each other in 1935." Max concealed his astonishment that the slim young beauty of that era was now, alas, an obese matron, middle-aged and devoid of any trace of the girlish fresh radiance that had attracted him to her. He introduced his wife as the two women assessed each other discreetly.

Mella invited Max and Shirley to her home for the following evening. She related the sad tale that her husband had left the country without divorcing her, although he knew the law of the land prohibited a wife from initiating the decree. This male prerogative that kept her legally attached, deprived Mella of the chance to remarry. She contented herself with a career and the pleasure of good children who were, themselves, happily wed. During the evening's visit, the Neumans were shown an album of photographs which included several of Mella and Max together at a beach, 26 years earlier.

*　　　　*　　　　*

By 1935 the atmosphere in France, indeed in all of Europe, was changing. Max observed this when he came back from his sojourn in Palestine. The sweetness of life was noticeably less sweet, even for those fortunate enough to have remained untouched by the Great Depression which sickened and weakened the world of capitalism. Many foresighted people already had a sense of foreboding and a somewhat acrid taste where once the tongue had known only honey. Besides losses in business investments, and vast unemployment among workers, there were increasingly ominous political signals. But people still frequented their favorite cafes and talked, laughed, and drank. A circle of artists were some of Max's friends. They were more concerned with selling a painting than in anything else. Often the immediacy of obtaining a few hundred francs meant the difference between meeting the landlady's demand for the rent money and being out on the street. Many times Max came to the aid of a desperate companion who considered loans he made as debts of honor and always repaid them.

A great deal of "shared distribution" took place: the artist who suddenly sold a few canvases never thought of putting anything aside for the lean days, but was always eager to pay for drinks and supper for the entire circle of friends. There was a tendency to ignore threats to groups, the nation, Europe, and to the whole world, among these young people involved in their "togetherness" and the group loyalty. Thus, there was an awareness, to be sure, of the advance of fascism and totalitarianism in the nations surrounding France but also a strong propensity to push it aside, hoping it would somehow go away. Max was pulled in the two directions: one that dictated an unchanged course to his life, and the other that whispered louder and louder, "become alert to increasing perils." Settling down after his successes in the Maccabi games and in his social life while in Palestine, he continued to work at the Rubinstein Institute. At times he would absent himself from there to "moonlight" at other jobs. It began when Max and a few friends began to sell radios. A territory that consisted of small country towns outside of Paris, where electricity was new provided wonderful opportunities to sell these little marvels of entertainment and communication to simple peasants. Reveling in the challenge of influencing sales-resistant prospects, Max often succeeded even in neighborhoods where power lines did not yet exist! He convinced farmers and small village tradesmen that it would give them status among their peers to be ready to plug in these small instruments of amazing sound the moment electric cables were installed. "I happen to know it is going to be very soon," he added for that final push. Earlier, when he was only 17 or 18 he had begun to test his talents as a salesman and knew that whenever he took up selling or "jobbing," he would have no trouble increasing his financial resources. It also built up his confidence to find out he was not really dependent upon his family—that he could make his own way when he chose to do so or when necessity demanded it—a situation that became a reality one day.

As the mood of the political atmosphere sobered, Max grew more intense in his activism. In 1936, with other members of *l'Association Contre le Racisme et l'Antisemitisme*, he joined the International Brigade in Spain, which consisted of young men of many nations who volunteered to fight with the Spanish Republican Army trying to prevent its government from becoming a fascist dictatorship. Those who knew how highly motivated Max was in the struggle of this cause, and what skills he had acquired while in the military and as a member of BETAR, urged and encouraged his participation. That is, all but Mme. Rubinstein. *Tante Helene* lectured him firmly, stating in conclusion that if he left to go to Spain there was no longer a place for him at the Institute. This ultimatum notwithstanding, Max went to fight in the civil war of Spain.

Supporters of the Republic arranged a special train leaving Paris with several thousands of volunteers, young men of varying political philosophies from humanitarian and religious to flaming communists and anarchists. Most were members of groups that reflected these diverse ideologies. All were bent on stemming the swelling tide of fascism, with its absolutism and its atheism, which was attempting to flow over republics and benign but weak monarchies throughout the European continent. Jews of political literacy sensed a particular urgency to take a stand on the issue in the battlefields of Spain, seeing the dire threat to their own people through the spread of the fascist doctrine. If Franco succeeded, it would augment the increasing strength of Adolf Hitler.

When the trainload that included Max reached its destination in Barcelona, parades were organized and the men marched to the martial music of rousing bands. The streets were filled with cheering civilians all responding wildly to the inspiration stirred by these foreign troops who were lending much-needed support to the attempt to save the Republic of Spain. The marches were meant to furnish comfort and to bolster confidence, which they did. Unfortunately, confidence—while a most important factor—is not sufficient to bring a military confrontation to a successful conclusion.

There in Barcelona the volunteer recruits were subjected to the pressures of "courtship" as each group of special interest politics sought members for its own battalions. Max settled into the Andre Marty 13th Battalion which was sent to a training camp near Albaceta. After several weeks the trainees went to Casa del Campo, near Madrid, where fierce and desperate fighting was in full swing. After awhile he was moved to Andujar, in the region of Cordoba, and the bitter battles of el Fronte de Lopera. The men of the International Brigade fought with the same dedication and vigor as did the Spaniards at their side. But it was a rag-tag army which, though made up of true idealists, also included all sorts of malcontents, misfits, and "losers." The counteraction to fascism was fragmented by the various factions with their quibbling, quarreling and their competitiveness. Too often they concentrated more upon triumphing over one another than upon the common enemy—the well-trained and well-equipped armies of Francisco Franco. The numerous groups with connections to the Soviet Union, still jostling and

86

elbowing for positions of power in the mother country, brought their conflicts to the battlefields of Spain. This splintered and weakened the Republican cause. Also, their in-fighting alienated would-be supporters in other countries, negating many chances for additional help the Republicans needed to succeed. Max lent his personal support for six months but then returned to France, disenchanted with the "Don Quixote" performance to which he had attached himself. Unquestionably he would one day have to fight on his own beloved French soil, he brooded.

On his return Max went through a period of de-emphasis in his political interests. His concerns grew more personal and to include attention to the development of his business skills. It was time to deal with his emancipation in terms of complete responsibility for self-support, despite the stipends he was receiving from his parents and from Helena Rubinstein. He turned to the textile industry which was flourishing in France. Without capital he was limited to easing himself into a middleman's position—a jobber. To retail merchants he sold fabrics that he bought from the wholesalers, a procedure involving little more than the exchange of money. After taking orders from merchants, Max placed his requisitions with the wholesalers who then shipped the textiles directly to Max's customers. There was a substantial differential between the two prices, and the incipient entrepreneur was confident he was on his way to becoming a successful businessman. It helped to avoid thinking about the nation's growing concerns over the growth of national socialism in Spain, Italy, and Germany.

By 1937 there was a decided and unavoidable unease. In that year Max became acquainted with several Indian Oxford-educated students who came to France to research the history and writings of the period before and during the French Revolution. One in particular, a Dr. Goswani, became a close friend of Max's. Not long after, when Dr. Goswani returned to his own country, he became a significant leader of India's ultimately successful fight for independence. The Indian was limited in his understanding of the French language, particularly the somewhat archaic language of the 18th century writings. Max and Dr. Goswani spent hours at a time in the National Library, as together they pored over the volumes of material that the Frenchman helped the Indian to translate for use in the revolution the doctor and others were preparing, for the independence of India. Max could reconstruct the words and phrases into a more simple French, within Dr. Goswani's grasp of the language. From this, the student wrote his own material both in English and in Hindustani, material that was intended to stimulate and motivate the Indian people to action. Although it was not until 1947, ten years later, that this part of the British Empire wrenched itself from the stubborn grip of its rulers, Dr. Goswani had the certain conviction it was inevitably India's future to become a free and independent nation.

The young doctor of philosophy urged Max to come to India with him when he returned. A man of vision, he foresaw the conflagration soon to burst forth in Europe, and he tried to persuade Max to save himself from its consequences. Goswani was ablaze with evolutionary fever and sought to entice Max through verbal pictures of the glorious romanticism of the fight to overthrow the forces of imperialism. Dr. Goswani described his country as a vessel of despair through starvation. Its contents, however often it was filled, and filled again as poor workers exhausted themselves for the benefit of those who employed them they were endlessly robbed, and avariciously drained by the unquestionable British thirst for wealth and power. Virtually nothing remained for the rightful beneficiaries, the native Indians. "You will be a part of that noble cause, my good friend," urged Dr. Goswani. But once more the seductive charisma of his beautiful city of Paris was successful in keeping Max clutched to her possessive breast. He did, however, accept an invitation to visit Madras and stay in the family mansion of the Goswanis. There, Max continued to help the inspired revolutionary. The two young men spent a good deal of the next six months on further translations and analyses of French revolutionary literary and historical texts and documents. It was a regretfully day for Dr. Goswani when Max left. Also, not long after returning to France, Max was discomforted by the realization that India could have been a haven for him as he saw a death web enclosing him.

Chapter Six
I'm A Fractional
Character

By 1938 Hitler's expansionism included—by means of the Munich pact—the shameful rape of Czechoslovakia. Hitler, Daladier, and Chamberlain met in Munich in the summer of 1938. The French and British diplomats appeased for the moment the hunger of Germany by handing over what did not belong to them: the Sudetenland of Czechoslovakia. After that, only the deluded or naive could no longer assess the insatiability of Hitler's nationalistic appetite. That year it was decreed in France that no man of military age and fitness would be allowed to leave the country without special permission. Max regretted his rejection of the numerous opportunities he had declined since 1935. Palestine, India, London, New York, Belgium and Switzerland all had been available to him in the three years before the edict of the autumn of 1938.

As an air force reservist Max was called at the first mobilization. After a training brush-up of about four weeks the men were then demobilized, but put on notice to remain "on the ready." September 3, 1939 both France and England declared war on the Axis, the combined governments of Germany, Italy, and Japan. This was two days after Hitler's armies marched into Danzig, then without difficulty continued brashly and boldly eastward into Poland.

To say that France was ill-prepared is to understate the situation. There was a large source of manpower, to be sure, but with little equipment at its disposal. And most of that was resurrected from WW1 leftovers, much mechanically impaired, all of it obsolete in terms of technological developments. Artillery was horse drawn! Max was trained for the air force that had few planes! Most of the men in the air force had never been off the ground although technically speaking they were to be ready to take to the air. Grouped close to the Belgian border the troops lived with the illusion that the neutrality of Belgium would insulate them from the likelihood of combat against the armies of the Third Reich. Eight months later, on May 10th the debacle occurred. During the interval, discipline grew lax, and combat procedures were reduced to virtual childlike games. Thus, caught off guard, poorly trained and meagerly equipped, the platoons were swept as by a tidal wave, in the enemy penetration that preceded the surrender of France by Marshall Petain.

The Germans thundered forward in hot pursuit of the fractured ranks of fleeing Frenchmen. Their tanks and their machine guns scoured the ground while the Luftwaffe sprinkled its charges of death and destruction upon soldiers and the civilians intermingled on all the routes, headed south of the Ardennes.

In a few weeks there was nothing more than the official transfer of administrative and military authority from the vanquished to the victorious. All of northern France was to be considered the occupied territory of the Third Reich; the southern part, separated from the north by the Loire River remained as a "Free Zone" until 1942, and was known as "Vichy France." In the latter years of the war Vichy also was designated as Nazi occupied territory.

Between the commencement of the war in September,

and the capitulation of France to Germany in May, Max's personal life changed significantly. December, shortly before Christmas—the war had been in progress for over three months—Max was in Paris on a leave. He noted how the character of the "Saturday Night Parties" had changed: they were more subdued, or there was an obvious forced gaiety that was even more sad than sadness. Many old friends were absent but one hesitated to inquire about an absentee lest the answer reveal another tragic consequence of the war. Food and wine were less plentiful. Uniformed men filled the rooms where young people met on the weekend for whatever diversion and comfort being together could afford them. The men who wore civilian clothes were defensive and uncomfortable, and they talked pointedly of their non-military war efforts. Their eyes looked hauntingly and beseechingly for signs of mitigation and approval from the others. The women clearly bestowed their favors upon congregants in uniform.

After his first Saturday evening of the December leave Max avoided these parties. The next week he went, instead, to the apartment of a young married couple, friends of long-standing and closeness. Emilie came to the door in response to his ring. She and Max exchanged effusive greetings, then led the way to sitting room. As the two entered Max saw another guest. It was a fair-haired girl, the fiancee of Roger Paget. The three: Max, Roger, and Ginette Mittnacht had shared many camping trips as members of the Touring Club of France, which comprised young men and women who were devotees of outdoor activity. Now Ginette was in an obviously advanced stage of pregnancy. In an even voice but with sad and candid eyes the girl responded to Max's inquiry about Roger by relating that he had been killed almost at the inception of the fighting, in September. There had been no time for a marriage to take place, mobilization came so quickly. Roger was sent to the front and to his death before he could marry his pregnant fiancee.

It was almost midnight when Ginette indicated her departure. Max offered to escort her home, and she said she would be pleased. When they reached her apartment she was not disinclined to his suggestion that they extend the conversation for a little while longer. She lived alone, Ginette told Max, and she had a successful career as an industrial designer and draftsman for the Peugeot motor car company. She showed Max a series of recent sketches, examples of her astonishing skills and ingenuity in automobile design. Max also noticed the subtle elegance, the graciousness of the apartment; instinctively he yielded to its charisma.

Perhaps it was the drifting mellowness of a late hour's quiet words in an amiable setting. Maybe the lure of the romantic and unexplored relationship. Or the vulnerability of a young soldier who perceives his country's—and his own—diminishing chance to avoid the conquest of the overpowering armies of the Third Reich, and the consequences. That same night Max offered Ginette a solution to her situation that she saw no reason to decline. He made a proposal of marriage! Once again he was about to marry out of his faith; Ginette was a Lutheran. He had so little confidence in the likelihood of surviving the war. It would be doing a good turn to provide this young woman with a legal husband to give her child a name and to financially aid her with the family allowance. Ginette would be "rescued" from the humiliation to herself and her very conservative family which an illegitimate birth would occasion. For Max the quid pro quo was that as the father of two children, rather than just one, he had a higher priority for transfer to a post more remote from the front lines of fire. More frequent leaves and weekend passes were another attractive "fringe" benefit of his magnanimous and chivalrous gesture, went the self-reasoning. A final glass of cognac sealed the pledge.

The next evening, Sunday, Ginette and Max went again to see Emilie and to reveal the news of their briefest of brief courtships! The two women and Max talked until late into the night. When the affianced couple rose to leave, their hostess offered them overnight accommodations in her spacious apartment. With her own husband absent in the war Emilie was often very lonely, particularly during the long dreary cold winter nights. Paris was colder and drearier than ever with heating fuel in short supply by this time. Ginette glanced at Max and he nodded in assent. In short order the bride/mother-to-be drifted into restful sleep in the guest room, unaware that Max was responding to Emilie's invitation to share her own bed. Their love-making was subdued and restrained. Quietly, Max explored her slender, small-breasted body, and soon they found mutual satisfaction before he crept back to the single bed in the sewing room which had been designated for him.

Early next morning, Monday, Ginette telephoned her supervisor at Peugeot. She would not report for work until after lunch. No, she was not unwell, she assured him, but an urgent matter would detain her all morning. She would explain when she came to work at two o'clock. A cold sharp wind lashed their faces as the couple hurried to the city hall to register for the marriage license which had to be followed by a three days' wait. Later in the week Ginette and Emilie appeared with Max and his friend Salek Goldberg at the city hall for the short, perfunctory civil formality that made Max and Ginette husband and wife. The four young people were joyful and casual, for no one could foresee that Salek would soon meet a tragic end.

The next year, 1940 when the German occupation began, Salek, an immigrant from Crakow, Poland made the decision to do business with the Nazis. As a furrier he supplied well-made, beautiful furs to officers and their wives. Salek was very kind and generous to Ginette during those months of thriving business activity, providing scarce food from the black market to his family and to his friends, which included Max's wife. Unobtainable food for a baby's need was one of the treasures Ginette received for her recently born little son from Salek Goldberg who was making practical use of his windfall of profits. But Max's warning to distrust the Nazis went unheeded. Ultimately, when his stock of furs was depleted and the Jews of Paris were rounded up and deported, Salek met the same fate as other Jews. The eager businessman who had carried on a thriving commerce with the enemy was not exempt from a concentration camp and death. On May 14th, 1941 over 3700 foreign male Jews were issued summonses, were arrested, and sent to detention camps.

After their wedding Max and Ginette spent the week-end together in Ginette's apartment; shortly before meeting Ginette Max had given up the apartment on Faubourg-St. Honore and stored his personal effects. Now her apartment became his home as well. Max returned to his barracks, then, a week later he was granted a "leave of compassion" for his fatherhood. Ginette named her boy Daniel Gerard. Just as had happened six years before—except that Claude was his natural son—Max married and became a father within a matter of days. A strange situation which was not likely to happen twice, actually did!

          *   **   **

In the spring of 1940 the German troops overcame France as deftly as a determined youth "de-flowers" an unsuspecting maiden. The attempt to fend off the advancing Teutonic armies from May 10th to June 17th was ineffectual. The retreat from the Ardennes, a dense forest region on the Belgian border, where Max was stationed, was nothing short of a rout. The French armies were forced further and further south, to the Loire region, with the Germans in feverish pursuit.

June 18th, over loud speakers came the report that Marshall Petain had agreed to a cease fire. Honorable, humane treatment was assured for all military personnel who capitulated. "Surrender yourselves and your weapons, remain in your compound," were the orders in essence. This was immediately followed by the commencement of erection of barbed wire fences to insure obedience and compliance.

Max's assessment of his personal situation as a Jew in a now Nazi regime, prompted him to take a less passive course of action. Leaving behind most of his military equipment, except for the uniform he was wearing, he scaled a part of the newly erected wall of the compound not yet installed with barbed wire. He fell in with the hordes of people crowding the roads. Some headed north, some south, many piled into all sorts of vehicles: military and civilian; most, however, set out on foot. There were other soldiers, old men and women, women with children, young men who—for various reasons had not been part of the armed forces. All were burdened with bundles, boxes, cases.

The weather was warm and as Max fled along the route north to Paris, he shed the heavy army jacket in which he had left his company. Besides, he was less conspicuous in just tan trousers and shirt, from which he removed the insignia. Now he aroused less curiosity as he mingled with the civilian men on the road. Gradually he destroyed some identifying cards and papers as he moved along. At night he slept in ditches, well out of sight of army patrols. In three days he was in Paris.

Confusion and fear swept over that city, like the menacing waters of a tidal wave. People looked grave, fearful, uncertain, but many had already dug in to endure whatever edicts of The New Order might be forthcoming, in a "go-with-the-flow" mentality. Some instinctively fled to smaller towns or to the countryside where they sought--what they hoped would be--a haven from too much regimentation and restriction, and where there were sources of food. They reasoned they might suffer less from prospective shortages of produce, dairy products and meat, as well as other supplies conquering armies usually requisition for their own use, without regard for the needs of the conquered civilians.

When Max arrived at the 20th Arrondissement, the district of Ginette's apartment in *Rue Etienne Marey*, he found the apartment abandoned and locked. He went to the concierge to find out where Ginette was. She had taken Daniel, their five month old baby and gone to Decize, near Nevers on the Loire River, Max learned. It was close to the home of Ginette's father and stepmother. The next day Max would go to Decize where his wife was living in a pension--a room and board arrangement--at the home of a farmer about three-quarters of a kilometer from her family.

But first, with the deliberateness of one without options, Max destroyed papers, books, documents, and any object that could identify him as a Jew, as an anti-fascist who had served in Spain with the Republicans, or as a Zionist. All this potentially damaging material was ferreted out of drawers, boxes, shelves. Everything was burned or otherwise rendered unrecognizable. Nothing was to be permitted to remain as a silent betrayer in the event of a search of his home. Already a Gestapo headquarters was situated directly across from the apartment building and this in itself was a chilling happenstance.

Late in the day Max Neuman left the house and made his way along the silent, uneasy, darkened streets of the neighborhood. He went to the home of Roger Sardou. Sardou was of a very old French family of writers. He and Max had been confreres in the days of their conscription service. An atmosphere subdued, somber and conspiratorial greeted Max as he entered the familiar surroundings of his friend's home. But there was the usual air of hospitality: a glass of cognac, some bread and cheese, and a steaming mug of coffee were brought to the table as Max and Roger sat opposite each other to confer. Although the air of that early summer evening was balmy Max felt an ominous chill, and was comforted by the food and drink.

The two talked for perhaps two hours and then were joined by a third man who brought the latest information regarding the developing administrative network of the Paris underground movement already rapidly beginning its resistance activities. The three talked of the caches of armaments, food, medical supplies, communications equipment and personnel, presently available for their operations. They discussed "safe" quarters for the thousands of men and women rallying to become part of the brave and determined obstructionists who were to utilize innovative as well as traditional methods to foil the Third Reich interlopers.

Tomorrow Max would go to Decize to bring Ginette and Daniel back to Paris where Max could slip home for a few hours at a time while he remained in the city carrying out his perilous work in and around the capital city. Tonight he would fall into a troubled fitful sleep on Roger Sardou's couch.

Max had left his army unit without official sanction and he had not—nor would he report to any German or French collaborationist military or civilian authority. Irreversibly a fugitive, he allied himself with the Resistance Movement. Later he defied edicts mandating registration to obtain a ration card, filing for a new identity card that carried prominently the designation *Juif*, "Jew," and ultimately the requirement to wear an arm band bearing the Star of David, also with the name Juif, which was intended to be a modern day mark of Cain.

In the gray light of dawn that struggled through the drawn blinds of the small room where Max spent the previous five restless hours, he rose from the couch and dressed again in the blue gabardine slacks and striped silk shirt he had changed into before coming to Sardou. His mind was clouded by insufficient rest but he willed it to function as his plan unfolded for making his way to Decize. There the reunion with Ginette and the baby was frenetic, then with little delay the three made the trip back to Paris.

Max's induction into the maquis—the underground resistance—followed a series of interviews and interrogations, interspersed with consultations within the leadership, investigation into his military and civilian activities and associations, finally concluding with his acceptance. An important consideration involved assessment of his anticipated behavior under conditions of torture, which was a likelihood following possible capture. If an inductee knew he would not, or could not endure the sadistic and barbarous methods used to extract information he must pledge himself to suicide This was to be accomplished by biting down on a cyanide capsule fastened to the gum line of the mouth. Many men and women determined to resist until they died of tortures rather than to take their own lives. They had to submit to the torture tests meted out by the maquis to measure their levels of tolerance.

Right from the outset Max said he judged himself incapable of enduring excesses of pain and that he elected to use the cyanide capsule if he fell into enemy hands. The maquis officer said to him: "Hold out your left hand with your fingers splayed." Max did as instructed. The other man placed a metal instrument between two fingers and another between the next two fingers; he squeezed Max's hand with a vise-like crushing motion. The recruit cried out and felt himself losing consciousness. Quickly, spirits of ammonia were waved under his nose and shakily he drank the glass of cognac handed to him. The interviewer laughed good-naturedly as Max revived. "In case you ever have any second thoughts about your choice. Now off to the 'dentist,'" he concluded as he indicated the room where Max would have the cyanide capsule fitted into place in his mouth. Max never harbored any doubts about how he must behave if the misfortune of becoming a captive were to befall him.

In countless acts of heroism thousands of men and women pledged their lives to the cause; they all lived quietly in their agony and obscurity, and many died. Blowing up or dis-railing trains carrying troops and supplies, dynamiting arsenals or provisions depots, attacking sentries, knocking out radio signal equipment, and a lengthy list of other acts of sabotage led to slowdowns and disruptions for the *Boches*. There were not only abundant casualties among the Resistance fighters but even among non-affiliated civilians who were executed in reprisal. Max remembered the remorse and pain that was felt particularly by members of the maquis who came from a particular village that suffered the loss of some fifty inhabitants as retribution. They had not revealed--had not even known—the identities of partisans who demolished rails that ran through their fields and had put out of commission several cars of a freight train. If the death of a German soldier occurred, from 10 to 50 people had to pay with their lives for the act. There were whole villages that were destroyed along with their populations after a successful and fruitful Resistance operation.

The groups in the Resistance generally comprised about 20 people. Frequently a member was moved to another group to fill in ranks decimated by casualties or out of need to keep knowledge and information fragmented and cryptic. Code names were used; Max was known merely as "Pierre," a name he adopted thereafter as of informal alter-identity. A counterfeit identity card gave his complete name as "Pierre Chanceux."

The work of "Pierre" during his period in the Resistance was principally as a saboteur of troop and supply trains. Loosening rail junctures, fastening plastic explosives were two very common assignments with men, munitions, and food supplies moving through the French countryside. The men of the maquis worked in pairs, often walking 6 to 8 kilometers to hide in forests and high brush, performing the assigned function, then returning to report its effectiveness to the group commander.

Frequently Max traveled from group to group dispatching messages. These were fragments of intelligence which, when pieced together with fragments brought by other workers had vital meaning. No one was entrusted with more than an indecipherable portion. The messages were either in writing or had to be memorized and recited orally to the intended recipient.

Trains moving across the countryside, through fields and vineyards, past farmhouses, barns, churches and schools often transported the victims of Nazi ideology and policy, and French acquiescence, or at least to be more charitable —timidity.

For a half-century one particularly excruciating memory of a sight Max witnessed lay deeply buried, its compelling pain like a festering wound that resisted nature's power to heal: a lengthy train was filled with Jews who were rounded up that year, 1941, bound for deportation to Eastern work camps and death camps. The men were in some cars, women in others, and the children herded together in cars devoid of adults. As one carload of children came into view Max saw crowded at the open windows the thin pale faces, the pleading troubled eyes. Slender, puny arms reached out, and he heard the anguished voices of these tiny helpless creatures: *"M'aidez, m'aidez!"* Help me, help me!

But they were beyond help, certainly beyond Max's power to alter the situation. The flood of his emotions —heart-wrenching sadness, rage, the frustration of his impotence—were all but paralyzing. And then, as his training and instincts demanded, he moved on with his assignment which was the delivery of a portion of a vital message.

One day, in 1991, as Max watched a TV program which depicted the Holocaust his face tightened, tears welled up in his aged eyes, they slowly drifted through the crags in his cheeks. In a trembling voice, breaking intermittently, Max haltingly related the episode of the children as he recalled the images.

*   *   *

Farmhouses were the most usual quarters for housing the underground workers. No one knew whether the people running a farm were actually farmers loyal to the Resistance and cooperating out of sympathy for the cause, or pledged members of the Resistance acting under the guise of farmers. No one knew anything about anyone else. To know was to place a greater risk on oneself and others. Everyone lived under a cloud of suspicion, for the fear and concern were very real that anyone might be an infiltrator from among the ranks of spies, opportunists, mercenaries, and dedicated fascists—both German and French.

Not only were overturned trains, trucks and convoys disruptions to the progress of the German war machine, but when not completely exploded, they contained supplies vital to the maquis. They supplemented the materials that the Allied forces made available for the underground operations through parachute drops and other surreptitious successful means. Unfortunately, many deliveries were not fulfilled, as one attempt after another aborted. Thus, it was only spasmodically and undependably that the Resistance received weapons and cartridges, communications materials, bulletins with guidelines for the formation and organization of groups, instructions for precautionary measures to take to guard against infiltrators, and explanations of guerrilla fighting techniques: both offensive and defensive training that included hand-to-hand struggles.

Manuals in survival were sent too, so that where little or no materials existed, members would have knowledge of trapping animals for food, fishing, and finding wild vegetation, as well as how to administer first aid to oneself or a comrade. The groups carried out "war games" as a means of gaining experience and proficiency. A cultural exchange between groups was a very necessary activity. It served as diversion, but also to overcome people's tendency to dislike one another because of superficial differences such as regional dialects and the varieties of lifestyles and tastes of the men and women from all ✡over France and from all strata of society. Couriers tried to bring news of successes and failures of the course of the war, or concerning specific battles and campaigns. The isolated groups were often close to despair and hungered for any scrap of morale-boosting information.

Maquis headquarters in England was the main lifeline. Valiantly the planes from there attempted to cover the network of groups waiting for parachutes that were the purveyors of materials. Pilots had to deviate their routes when threatened by German attacks, which meant that a planned flight was always uncertain. When a group in rural France identified an allied plane, recognized by its sound, it signaled by lighting a small fire or by operating a torchlight to indicate the group's location. To confuse the enemy, decoy fires and signals would be used to deflect German patrols on the "lookout." The most important piece of equipment was the radio. A captured radio station was replaced within a half hour by a back-up station from other equipment ready to be put into service.

Besides the "sworn" members, couriers were recruited from every possible source, and even school children on bicycles served to transmit coded messages from group to group or from a radio station to a field group. Special groups were pledged to the singularly defined function of killing Gestapo officers in order to prevent German operations, to avenge fallen or captured Resistance workers, or simply to demoralize the enemy.

*   *   *

For months Max was posted in, and near Paris, quartered there and engaged in activities that made it possible to make short unannounced visits to his home and wife. During one of these meetings a child was conceived, unplanned and unexpected. When the little girl of Max and Ginette was born they called her Christianne Madeleine, a deliberately non-Jewish name. It was in May 1941, and the peril of being a non-Aryan was unmistakable and looming greater and greater every day.

Soon after that Max was sent to Dordogne, and he moved his little family to Perigueux, the prefecture of the region. France was still divided into an "Occupied Zone," and "Vichy," the free zone—a term which was almost from its inception an ironic euphemism. Dordogne was in Vichy. It became an important center of Resistance activity, remaining so until it, too, became Occupied Territory after the Allied landings in North Africa and the Germans needed to secure their position in the south of France.

Often Max was obliged to cross back and forth through the well-patrolled Demarcation Line that separated these two political divisions of France. His intense fear of being recognized and denounced increased as this kind of activity resulted in so many deaths among members of the maquis. Under conditions of torture and with captors' assurance they were buying their lives some of the captured men and women revealed names of their comrades. Sufficient desperation and delusion understandably led them to believe they could save themselves. When they did comply, both the informant and those whose identities they revealed were executed. Various missions were aborted through information thus extracted.

One time just after crossing into the Occupied Zone, laden with food supplies for posts in Paris Max was encountered by a former friend, a Frenchman and an Aryan, but of socialist propensities, and consequently unlikely to be favorably disposed to the control of his country by the fascists. Even so Max felt the cold clammy sweat of terror and panic over this unexpected chance meeting with one to whom he was recognizable. The eyes of the other man looked haunted and frightened. The two exchanged a few stilted words and hurried away from each other. It was a time to be anonymous, for anyone was a potential danger. Always, for the rest of his life, Max retained the watchword he adopted during those times: *vivant heureux, vivant cache !* "living happy is living hidden." Despite the wisdom of this prudent philosophy he continued to be a person who defended his strong convictions and principles, sometimes fearlessly, but even while in fear of his personal safety.

Chapter Seven
I Must Flee To Fly

From the time reports out of London told of the formation of regiments of "Free French," under the inspiring leadership of General Charles de Gaulle, Max was determined to join these fighting forces stationed in England. After 18 months in "La Resistance Interieure"—which distinguished the resistance from the Free French Force connected to the Royal Air Force in England and in North Africa—Max decided to attempt an escape from France. Late in 1941, just around the time the United States entered the war he requested to be released from the maquis.

"Day by day my life was in increasing danger. I was frustrated, too, by the greater uncertainty of the outcome of each of our missions of spying and sabotage, as well as the discouragement over the shortage of the most basic supplies. What was also of great concern and dismay to me was that my visits to my wife and my children—though clandestine—were putting them at risk. Ginette's landlady as well as a few nearby neighbors were aware of my periodic presence. Admittedly, they had all been confirmed to be extremely hostile to the invaders. Many, even though not formal maquis members were fully cooperative in making their homes and their farm buildings supply hideouts and places of refuge for resistance members. They frequently passed information or significant clues of what they observed, and curious incidents that aroused their suspicions concerning German activity in the region. Still, their knowledge of me constituted a danger.

"But I was being pulled in two directions: I wanted to leave; I

knew it was the best thing to do. At the same time I was faced with my wife's adamant protest against this. She kept urging me to stay, to remain close to her and our very young children."

Separating himself from the maquis demanded mutual trust; the leadership of the unit had to be certain a man or woman who left the unit did not become a source of betrayal. With underground ranks continually infiltrated, many members lost their lives because of defectors. Significant operations were frequently aborted as information was passed to the Germans and to the collaborating French authorities from their agents working the ranks of the underground resistors, or former members.

Max, too, had to make a decision to trust his unit leaders. He needed to feel certain that there really was absolute confidence that he was not deemed to be a security risk if released. Otherwise he might be authorized to leave and then "liquidated" before any presumed possibility of endangering the group. He had knowledge of plans, positions, names of men and women, of leaders as well as rank and file members. The Germans and their French collaborators would go to great lengths to obtain the information.

Max was granted clearance and a safe conduct pass to receive assistance from other Resistance units that would cooperate and offer assistance to his escape. He trusted the sincerity of the agreement of separation, but he was reluctant to give up the precaution of keeping the cyanide capsule wedged on the gum line of his mouth and considered waiting to remove it only when—and if—he succeeded in making it across the border into Spain. A live grenade was also harbored in his pocket. If captured by the French or German police he planned to fulfill his suicide pact and was determined to take his captors to death with him. Although he employed every resource at his disposal to outwit the enemy—training, skills, intelligence and survival instincts, the fugitive was well aware

108

of the strong possibility of being apprehended. Military and civilian authorities were not the only danger; bounty hunters were rampant.

In Dordogne Max bade farewell to Ginette and the children. From then until the liberation of France three years later there would be no communication, no knowledge of one another.

*   *   *

An unexpected incident occurred scarcely a week before Max was to attempt the escape. With the details and strategies being formulated, he valued the little time that was left to be with his wife, toddler son Daniel, and infant daughter Christianne. Ginette was distinctly unhappy—even reproachful—of his resolve to try to reach and join the armed forces in England.   Max was suddenly summoned to confer with his group leader about an assignment to assist a Jewish detainee to escape she and her baby were shipped to a camp outside of France. Gestapo agents rounding up Jews had missed casting their net over her young husband. He had been fortunate in avoiding capture, but after fleeing to safety, he learned that his wife and year-old son were now in a women's detention center, a temporary situation of uncertain time frame and ultimate outcome.

"How can I refuse?" Max retorted in an emotional exchange with his wife when he told her he had accepted one more assignment, but revealing nothing more than the barest outline of the purpose of the mission. Even what he did tell her was only to explain why he had to arise the next morning hours before daylight, and soundlessly leave through a window hidden from view by a woodshed.

The building in which the luckless women and children were being housed was situated in a country village. The women could circulate in the small town by requesting permission to leave the building for some specific errand such as to purchase a few items at the chemist, or even to give a fretful, restless child a brief release of feelings by taking a walk.

Max, a car, and a driver who was also a member of the Resistance group drove to a wooded area where the car and driver remained concealed while Max continued on foot to the women's detention center. Through means that had not been made known to Max the woman had been surreptitiously informed of the impending attempt to effect her escape.

Max posed as her cousin who had come to visit her. The two were to take a casual walk, the baby in his stroller, nothing with them that might suggest anything more. Playing their roles well, as their very lives depended on doing so, the two adults talked amiably as they moved out the door, along the streets, past shops, then a few houses, and finally to where the car and driver were stationed.

A cover of carpet on the floor of the car was removed. A recessed area barely large enough for the woman to crouch in was where she must remain for the length of the journey to the safe house where her husband—whose anxiety was almost beyond endurance—was awaiting a joyful conclusion to the nightmare. Max sat in the seat next to the driver, holding the baby who was bundled into a blanket. The men knew the climax of the drama was the danger upon reaching a Gestapo post they would have no way to avoid.

"You have the starring role in this scene, Pierre," the driver murmured to Max as the post loomed up in front of them. A Gestapo agent stepped out and lifted his rifle in a "halt" gesture. The men in the car, knowing the procedure produced their papers. The agent examined the documents, then nodded at the child indicating he was waiting for an explanation. "My sister's baby. He has been ill, and I had him to the doctor because my sister is herself unwell. Now I am bringing the child back home." In a nurturing gesture Max drew the blanket more closely about the little one' s head as a slight wind came up.

"It looks like a storm is on the way," Max squinted at the darkening sky. "Yes, yes, you'd better move along," the agent responded as he handed each man his papers, stepped back with a snap of his leather boots, and made a brief waving motion that signaled "pass." The car with its two men, the baby boy, and the concealed mother proceeded with the precarious journey to its happy ending. Whether that young family survived the entire period of the Nazi occupation Max could not know. All anyone could do then was to try to buy time, survive the crisis of the moment. One day the horror would be over. There had to be an end! There had to!

*   *   *

From Dordogne Max took a route south to Perpignan. He was aware of the clergy's activity in smuggling Frenchmen and foreigners out of the country into Spain. Contacting any one of these known sympathizers would be relatively safe.

There were a number of churches in Perpignan and Max went to the first one of the Protestant denomination he saw. He described to the pastor his experiences of the preceding 18 months, told that he was a Jew, married to a Protestant woman and that they had two children. He pointed out that he was in particular danger of not having registered since the collapse of the government, as was required by the Vichy and the German authorities, and had no way of obtaining rations by legal means. Although Max had brought with him money, gold coins and a diamond ring he would attempt to retain what he could for a time when it might be necessary to use these as a bribe in exchange for his life. He therefore appealed for help on humanitarian grounds, which he hoped the clergyman could provide. The pastor examined the safe conduct pass the maquis had issued Max, and said he could

111

attach him to a group of young men and women about to leave on one of the escape missions.

The pastor told Max that among the clergymen involved in this clandestine work, one of them was a rabbi. Max and the rabbi met and talked two or three times before Max's departure from Perpignan. At the appointed time Max set off with a small band of young people. They were instructed to take a train, then a bus and finally to walk along a designated route where they would be met by a guide when they reached Cerbere. Though all the directions were followed precisely the guide failed to appear and the mission was aborted. This was one of the frightening hazards, for one could not be certain that a contact had not been caught beforehand and forced to reveal details of the project, or might fear to fulfill it especially if he had any reason to believe someone had informed on him or suspected him. A would-be contact could even be replaced by an enemy agent and the fugitive(s) could be arrested by entrapment. Consequently any "hitch" in the plans threw one into devastating panic.

Not knowing why a guide had not appeared the group retraced the route it had taken and returned to Perpignan. As the young people left the train Max saw at a short distance from the station that two German soldiers were walking with a young man between them, apparently having taken him into custody. Max recognized the prisoner as someone he had seen in the office of the rabbi, working at a desk and among the files. Max watched as the handcuffed man flanked by the two Germans was led away.

Max hastened to the office of the rabbi who listened intently as Max related and described the incident he had just witnessed. Politely he asked to be excused saying he had an urgent conference and must close the office for the afternoon. A rim of pallor formed around his mouth, and his eyes were averted as he spoke and as he moved about the office collecting files of papers which he slipped into a pocket inside his coat. Max and the rabbi bade each other a good day as they left the office. The clergyman locked the door and hurried away. That evening when Max went to a cafe where he had met the man on two occasions he noted the rabbi was not among the patrons sitting at the tables. Nor was he seen anywhere in Perpignan, and Max felt certain that his warning could have helped the rabbi to flee for his own life, as he had helped others to do, and before his luckless assistant might betray him under the torturous questioning that broke many a loyal friend or associate.

A week passed and then came another chance for Max to move on from Perpignan. The pastor and his wife agreed to an arrangement that could include him in their plans. They were going to a small mountain village situated between Perpignan and Cerbere and could take with them one young person, very able-bodied who was able to walk as much as 30 kilometers of difficult terrain. Max leaped at the chance and was accepted. The three set out together on a bus to Cerbere. Just before departure the pastor assisted Max to remove the cyanide capsule, which had to be very carefully extracted, for even very small particles of that deadly substance were bound to make him quite ill if ingested. With the aid of a sharpened probe it was eased from along the gum, removed from his mouth and discarded.

Max, the pastor, and his wife all sat separately on the bus and did not communicate until they all got off at a small town. From there they walked through dark of night along rough and winding footpaths to a farmhouse in the mountains in a region set high with wide visibility of the surroundings and of valleys below. This made it relatively safe because anyone approaching the house could be seen well in advance of arrival. Informers had once alerted the authorities that it harbored a nest of the Resistance, but it was so strategically located that activities there managed to go on as before.

When the three arrived Max learned why the pastor and his wife had made the journey. Other people were waiting to be led by them into Vichy by way of Perpignan, people who had crossed from Spain into France and the couple had come to escort them. These were Spanish refugees, sought by the Franco regime for having fought in the Republican army during the Civil War. They were fleeing for their lives from their country, and seeking a haven in France. All the arrivals were given food and a place to rest. During the night the pastor, his wife and the Spaniards left the farmhouse. In a clearing a car was waiting to take them to Perpignan.

Later, a member of the farmhouse group led Max to where he would take a bus to Ceret. He was continuing southward. Before leaving him the man obtained the bus ticket for Max. Everything was done so that he had a minimum of contact with strangers whose curiosity could be aroused. The less anyone knew of you the greater were your chances to succeed. Nor did a fugitive such as Max want to know anything or anyone not directly concerned with his perilous effort. The people he had seen at the farmhouse, those being led to Perpignan, did not communicate with Max, nor he with them. "Ships that pass in the night," as the saying goes.

Max was now prepared to board the bus, get off in Ceret, then he was to remove a large white handkerchief from his pocket and wipe his face as if pausing to remove sweat and dust. This was the prearranged signal to his contact in Ceret to approach him and lead him to a safe house. As other passengers also left the bus and hurried away in all directions Max followed his instructions. It was twilight and the streets were emptying. No one came forward to meet him and Max grew frightened. The driver of the bus who had gotten out of it to help a few people remove luggage, boarded it again, probably to drive it to the garage. Max was alone. Terror—sheer terror, followed by a descent into panic! There was no way to return, for the bus would not leave again until the next day, and there was no alternate plan. Max sought obscurity in the shadows, trying to compose himself. He looked around him and saw a small church. He approached it, went to a side door that led to the rectory and he knocked. It was opened slightly and stealthily. Max had to take the risk of saying he was a stranger seeking refuge.

The pastor who answered the knock looked very fearful. "Run! Run away from here quickly, quickly," the man said hoarsely. "My church is unsafe. I am being watched, this place is under surveillance. You will be arrested here, go, go quickly to that inn." Max looked in the direction pointed out to him and saw the inn close by. "You will be helped," said the pastor as he shut the door swiftly.

Max did as he was told. He was quickly admitted when he reached the place, and immediately given a hot meal, a thick nourishing meatless stew, then a portion of roasted rabbit and huge chunk of bread, along with strong coffee. He was instructed to lie down with all his clothes and sleep until he would be awakened for a pre-dawn departure with some others. He fell into an exhausted sleep. He never learned why his contact did not appear, but it is most likely that he too was under surveillance or perhaps had been arrested. Before he fell asleep Max thought about the last hour which had included the anguish and despair of standing alone and visible to two German patrols who were walking in his direction as he stood wiping his face to signal the contact that never came. His hand had moved to his pocket, his fingers gradually circled around the grenade which was about to become his last hope for an honorable and least painful end to his young life. He knew he would have fulfilled his determination never to

115

surrender himself.

They left while darkness still cloaked them, the band of six men, three women—one the wife of a general who had already reached England—and two teenagers, the children of one of the women. The group was in the charge of a Basque guide who knew every centimeter of the area, as well as the routine of the field gendarmes and of the Spanish guardias.

They marched along single file and rapidly for several hours, up steep mountain trails to altitudes of 1800 to 2000 meters. The cold and the fast pace set by the guide were too much for the wife of the general, and the young men of the group, including Max took turns carrying her. When the guide brought the group to a halt he announced: "You are now in Spain and I do not go farther with you." From their vantage point on the mountain he pointed out a city below. He warned the escapees to avoid coming close to that village, then drew a rough sketch of the route they must take to work their way around it. He explained there were great numbers of Spanish border patrols who would arrest them for illegal entry into Spain. Or worse yet, they could fall into the hands of German patrols circulating the area in Spain that was not too far from the border between France and Spain, who would deposit them back in France where they would be turned over to the German authorities.

At that point Max made the decision to separate from the others believing that his chances to succeed were greater if he proceeded alone. He knew that the peasants of this region so close to France were usually conversant with the French language and that he would be able to make his way.

Late that night Max reached the outskirts of Figueras. He saw a country general store and cantina. Inside were soldiers and working men drinking and talking loudly. Exhausted, cold, hungry and thirsty, Max went in. He asked for a hot chocolate, the thick dark sweet Spanish drink that is so comforting and energizing. Though he spoke the words in Spanish the woman at the counter replied in a low voice in French, indicating by her use of his language that she must know he was one who had come over the border. She motioned him discreetly to the kitchen. He followed her unnoticed in the very dim light of the cantina, the public tavern. The woman's family was seated around a table eating and talking.

Two women rose from the table and brought food to Max, then someone bade him rest until the cantina was closed. When all the patrons had gone the youngest of the men seated at the kitchen table was chosen to lead Max through a fifteen to twenty minute walk along an obscure path where he could continue safely and find a safer place for the overnight stay. There were isolated farms and the people were all sympathizers. Seeing a light in a farmhouse about an hour's walk from where the boy had left him Max went to the door and knocked softly. A woman responded. *"Yo soy un escapado de Francia."* I am an escapee from France. He went on to explain that he was seeking to reach the British consul which was located in Barcelona. Then the woman ushered Max into a room where a younger woman was attending an old man lying in bed. Max was given blankets and invited to lie down in a corner of the room. Although Max rose with the first rays of the morning sun the family was already actively engaged. He drank the hot synthetic coffee that was offered him and left carrying a donation of a part of a loaf of homemade coarse corn bread, hard enough from age to be useful as a lethal weapon! He was nonetheless grateful.

In the villages and small towns in the countryside of northern Spain people were dependably sympathetic to a Frenchman in flight. Most of the Spaniards of the region had fought with—or at least supported—the Republican army against fascism and Francisco Franco. They were not kindly disposed toward their government's pro-German attitude which only technically retained a neutral position. With caution and discretion Max was able to obtain hot food and night shelter in places where he had to keep out of the way of the brutal Guardia Civil. The peasants had very little food, but their simple goodness impelled succor. Long afterward Max learned the extent of the sacrifice of someone who had gifted him with an egg! Lying at night in front of a still-warm baker's oven, on flour sacks heaped up to make a mattress eased the stress of his experience, and was usually preceded by a donated meal of freshly baked bread and hot coffee. For a 30 year old man in excellent health there was not yet a great deal of physical hardship to undermine his strength.

One day as Max made his way through a wooded area, he encountered a young fellow gathering wild mushrooms. After a short conversation an agreement was reached to have the man act as a guide toward the route to Barcelona, but with a wide circle around Gerona which was a Guardia headquarters and where Max would assuredly be arrested. The two walked along together for several hours, then the guide persuaded Max that it was safe to stop at a village cantina for a drink or two. It proved to be not at all safe; not long after leaving there he was arrested by a pair of guardias. Max thought his presence at the bar had attracted the attention and the interest of an informer. Now the consequences of that brief respite had to be paid. The two guardias lightened Max's possessions by taking his money, his cache of gold coins and a ring set with a large diamond. They escorted him to their headquarters. At this guard station, the first place to which he was taken, he was searched and interrogated. The search revealed nothing, of course, for the guardias had relieved him of his valuables and he was traveling without any form of identifying documents. This was done in accordance with maquis advocacy as their prescribed methods for escapees.

In the interrogation that followed the search Max declared he was a native of Palestine, hence a British subject, and was living in France. The charge was made against him of being an illegal entrant and Max was incarcerated in the prison of Gerona, although it was accepted that he entered Spain not for the purpose of residence but as a transit political escapee en route to join the British forces in Gibraltar, with the aid of the British Consulate. Most of the French captives declared themselves to be French-Canadians and the Spanish authorities came to know this as a ploy to avoid being sent back to France.

Because it was different, Max's statement was more convincing, and he was believed to be a Palestinian British subject. Immediately upon being conducted from Guardia headquarters to Gerona prison his internment began with a shower, having his head shaved, followed by a period of waiting, wrapped in a blanket while his clothes were put through a delousing process. The garments were returned to him greatly diminished in size by the heat and use of disinfectants. Then Max was led to his cell. Forty-nine other men were in the bare concrete room that would have been scarcely adequate for twenty. Men of various nationalities crowded around the new arrival, eager for news of the war. It was early in 1942 and Max could report the entrance of the United States into active fighting, a heartening note to these men in an otherwise cheerless situation.

The first week of imprisonment was extremely difficult, with many adjustments. There was a sense of relief, of course, that the escape had been accomplished. The trauma of all the dangers he had faced in the preceding eighteen months climaxing in these last days of flight were now floating about his consciousness in waves of conflicting emotions. They pressed aggressively and insistently upon his fatigued nervous system. With equal determination he prodded and herded

119

them into deep dark hidden cavities below the mind's awareness. More or less obediently they stayed there for 40 years, occasionally freeing themselves during those four decades, behaving like merciless little devils destroying endless chances for joy, security, love, and a sense of well-being. Not only did these "imps" of his psyche fail to fade away, they grew more ferocious and increased in number as the subsequent events of 1943, 1944, and 1945 accumulated.

Max's imprisonment over a period of nine months was followed by service as a combatant, presence at the war crimes trials in Nuremberg, and then a tour of duty for the United Nations Relief and Rehabilitation Administration (U.N.R.R.A.) in Germany—until 1946.

In addition to the effort to gain some of his emotional balance those first days, prison life also demanded struggles in the task of safeguarding his physical health and strength. Food and hygiene were minimal. The prisoners slept on pallets meagerly filled with straw. Each man was allocated a half-meter of width; they alternated head to feet At first Max had only the concrete floor and a thin blanket for a bed, but after a few days he was issued a pallet. For a week he had only the usual prison rations for nourishment: coffee and a small bread roll for breakfast, watery vegetable soup for the noon meal, and an orange in the evening. But the aura of camaraderie that existed among the men—and even with some of the guards—helped to dispel the pain of detention and of the deprivations of comfort and proper sustenance. Verbal communication among cell mates and even with prisoners in other cells was permitted. But sad and sobering was the view from the cell windows as each morning the foreign prisoners were witnesses to the executions of Spaniards, former fighters in the Republican army whose court appeals ultimately ran out and death sentences were carried out.

As the second week of prison life began for Max there was a visit from the British representative of the International Red Cross. He recorded the names of purported British subjects and made allocations of money that would prove to be means of preventing malnutrition and despair. Each man under his jurisdiction received 35 *pesetas* a week and a ration of 2 packs of cigarettes a week. A blanket and a set of underwear were provided; the extra undergarments enabled a British prisoner to change and launder his underwear and to have the comfort of two blankets during the cold nights when the men lay on scraps of straw which was all that was between them and a concrete floor.

Heavy smoker that he was, Max was aware of the importance of selling his cigarettes to buy food, or of trading them with Spanish prisoners for food their family members brought them when they visited. A prisoner who could spare one of the coarse crusty loaves of bread was eager to obtain cigarettes for it. Selling his cigarettes yielded 160 pesetas, which when added to the 35 pesetas allocated by the consul meant Max could visit the cantina each morning during the one hour exercise and recreation period. He bought oranges, hot chocolate or the warm watered-down milk that was available, and bars of *Torrones*, a sugary nougat.

Prison routine allowed two exercise periods each day. For one hour in the morning and again in the afternoon the men played soccer in the courtyard, did calisthenics, and socialized in the fresh air and sunshine. Those who spoke a little Spanish or who spoke French, which many of the Spaniards knew to some extent exchanged conversations with the Spanish political prisoners. Their sentences ranged from 30 years to life; some were condemned to execution. The foreign prisoners felt an obligation to do what they could to lift the morale of these doomed men. The foreigners knew they would one day be released when Allied countries to which

121

they belonged could exchange them for much-needed materials of which Spain had depleted itself during the Civil War.

The domestic prisoners received training to do art work: paintings and sculptures with religious themes. They were allowed to sell these, or give them to their relatives. Many secretly sketched scenes of the miserable prison conditions of maltreatment. The sketches were smuggled out with departing visitors and with foreign prisoners upon their release. Thus it was that even within an atmosphere of such harshness most of the men retained a semblance of civilized and compassionate behavior. British prisoners shared their cigarettes and their peseta allowance with non-British prisoners who had no such life sustaining supplements. But woe unto the prisoner who did not rely upon magnanimity and attempted to steal a portion of bread or a cigarette or any personal item belonging to another! Violent quarrels, even fist fights erupted that brought the guards on the run and ended in severe punishments to the participants. A man's clothing was rolled up to form his pillow at night and in that roll he kept everything he possessed in prison, including his shaving articles, comb, items of personal hygiene, cigarettes, money, and any crust of bread or other scraps of food kept for quieting the torments of hunger that often gripped a man during the night when he needed to sleep. The agony more than once caused Max to gnaw on a piece of his dirty blanket.

The routine varied only on Sunday when attendance at Catholic Mass was mandatory. As a band played the lively strains of the *paso doble* the men marched to an outdoor amphitheater where they received the religious ritual with varying responses of comfort, consolation, boredom or disdain.

Despite the harshness of their lives of deprivation, the prisoners did not manifest sociopathic behavior. On the contrary, there were any number of examples of cooperation and psychological reinforcement, and a desire to maintain the values of a civilized society, such as the pooling of money and cigarettes so that those who had a supplement from the British government were sharing it among all foreign prisoners. Everyone knew that the extra food the visitors of the Spanish prisoners brought and the little additional food one managed to buy at the canteen could make the difference between life and death. Even so, many men suffered dysentery and low grade infections due to mal-nourishment which left them weak in body and spirit.

Anguish and deep sorrow often overtook Max, for he watched from the cell window the sunrise execution of one, and another, and another of the young Spaniards with whom he had spent hours of recess periods in the courtyard. All were condemned but not told in advance the date of their execution. Max recalls the depth of his feelings when he saw some of these youths marched in front of the firing squad sometimes only a day after friendly and comradely words had been exchanged.

*   *   *

In May (1942) rumor had it that a deal had been struck between the government of Spain and the Allies as to the ransom that would be paid for the release of British, French, Canadians, Americans, and men of other nationalities. The Allied governments had been aggressively negotiating the release of the prisoners. The Spanish government, desperately in need of the materials that would accrue from the exchange showed great willingness to deal. But a critical situation arose involving the Spanish government and the German government. Spain's relationship with Germany was an impediment. Germany insisted that Spain detain all able-bodied men of military age.

In addition to the ransom Spain needed to contrive an

acceptable rationale for releasing all the men, therefore the Spanish Government maintained that the escapees and other prisoners were actually unfit for military service. This led to a stalemate which was causing a great deal of uncertainty about a successful conclusion to the negotiations.

Suddenly, the prisoners of Allied countries were removed from Gerona Prison and transported to a small resort town, Caldas de Malavella. There, during the weeks of continued negotiations they were allowed to circulate freely, but only within the limits of the town. Now, in a less confined area, and with prospects of imminent release, their spirits soared as they eagerly grasped at the rumors of an agreed upon exchange of men for wheat, phosphates and other necessities that Spain lacked. Local gossip also occupied attention among the idle men. There was talk of a notorious village priest whose greed and stinginess made him the subject of ridicule and contempt. Everyone knew the "padre" lived well and dined unstintingly but was, to say the least, quite uncharitable. Rising to a challenge, Max made a bet that he could induce the priest to offer him hospitality. The stakes were set. Max arrived at the doorway of the priest's cottage while the men who had bet against the success of his venture crouched near the open windows of the cottage to witness the encounter. Max rapped at the door and it was opened by a maidservant. She then called the priest and left the two men as the priest led Max into his study.

"Padre, I have a great need of some important information," Max began after the priest indicated he understood enough French to know what the prisoner might say. "What is it, my son. What seems to be troubling you?" "Padre, is it possible you could tell me what a diamond would be worth, a diamond the size of a hazel nut?" Max made a circle with his thumb and forefinger to emphasize visually the size of the gem under discussion. The priest's flabby moon face grew crimson and his eyes widened with excitement. "Maria," he shouted to the maid, clapping his hands loudly to summon her quickly. In rapid fire Spanish he gave her orders and she laid the table, bringing platters of ham, cheese, fresh bread and a jug of wine. The Padres efforts to contain his eagerness were monumental as he watched the starved prisoner wolf down provisions he had only dreamed of in the past four months.

When Max's appetite appeared to be appeased the priest spoke unctuously: "Now my son, show me this diamond of which you speak." With sham innocence Max looked earnestly into the gleaming eyes of the priest. "Padre, no, it is not that I have such a valuable treasure; it is only that IF it should be my good fortune to find one I want to know how many pesetas I might be able to get for it." Max was on his feet poised for the flight that only narrowly preceded blows from a broom the priest grabbed up from the corner of the room. The man lunged with fury and looked close to apoplexy Max thought as he glanced fleetingly over his shoulder while he retreated. He burst from the room, out the cottage door and ran swiftly along the footpath that led to the village. "Guardia, guardia," croaked the priest as he, too, went toward the town. Even the police officers who came in response to his indignant complaint could barely contain their mirth as ✡they listened to how the *estranjero*, the foreigner had defrauded him of a lavish meal.

Not far behind the shrieking priest pursuing Max with the flailing broom were the comrades who had made the bet and witnessed the scene inside the priests home. They emitted gales of laughter and shouted their astonishment to each other and conceded that losing the bet was well worth the loss of a week's ration of cigarettes to view such a scene. The anecdote spread through the ranks of prisoners and townspeople and Max was much admired for his courage and ingenuity. "Marco," as the Spaniards called him, became a folk hero.

The five or six weeks that the men remained in Caldas gave opportunities to build health and strength. The town was a health resort known as "The Vichy of Catalan," where rich Spaniards came to take the waters. Even though not permitted into the spas, the prisoners could bathe frequently in a pond just outside the town center. It was in the luxurious tourist hotel that the five hundred or more men were quartered. Although four or five occupied a room that normally accommodated one or two, the men were comfortable. For them it was luxury just to sleep in beds between sheets after the straw pallets of the Gerona prison.

Prisoners with money or tradeable items bought food and clothing, cognac and wine. Passes were issued routinely for the men to visit bordellos in Gerona. They went there by train and in the company of guards. Some of the men even took jobs with town tradesmen and earned money during their sojourn. This semblance of normal activity, the chance to be outdoors in the mild climate and to exercise vigorously kept Max and all the men physically and emotionally well. Nevertheless they could not for a moment forget that they were prisoners. All roads from Caldas were heavily patrolled to prevent escapes; the prisoners were warned that if any among them tried to flee the entire complement would be promptly returned to Gerona. This made each man an effective custodian of the detention of the others. At night the prisoners were securely locked into the hotel building, and beds were routinely checked for the head count.

The hopes and anticipation of release were dispelled when it was announced one night at bed check that at 8 a.m. the following morning they were to stand ready to depart Caldas by train, with no information made available about where they were being sent. Despondently they gathered their few personal effects and took their places in the courtyard for a breakfast of coffee, a roll, and an orange. Later, when their bundles were examined the Spanish guards laughed to discover each man had packed into his shirts and underclothes a pair of bed sheets. Good naturedly they allowed the theft, understanding how much this small comfort meant to the luckless foreigners. Max also packed bottles which he had filled with the mineral water, knowing its value to his health during time when pure water was in short supply.

From eight in the morning until three in the afternoon the men stood and waited for the administrative red tape to be untangled. All day there was nothing to eat or drink, nor was there anything as sustenance when they were crammed into box cars waiting on a side track. They were marched between close-order guardias whose rifles were cocked and at readiness to shoot any man who might break ranks in a possible attempt to make a run for it. At sundown they left. About midnight as the trains made a stop, members of the Spanish Red Cross came aboard. They passed out to each man an orange, a bread roll and a mug of hot coffee. At 2 or 3 o'clock in the morning a stop was made to allow the men, one boxcar at a time, to leave the train to relieve themselves in the fields. Armed guards, on the ready, surrounded. Before this official stop the men managed to urinate through a small opening between the wall of the boxcar and the door, where the lock and chain left a few inches of slack.

In whispers some of the men plotted an escape through the bottom of the car by ripping up a floor board. Two or three in Max's car made an unceremonious exit in this manner, with the rest of the men singing loudly and laughing to cover the sounds of the scramble to escape. It was accomplished when the train was turning slowly around a turn and the men could slip to the track beneath the train without injury.

The journey lasted 3 days and then the men were marched about six kilometers to the infamous concentration camp "Miranda de Ebro," in the province of Burgos. Max pondered an escape plan during the march. The guards who accompanied the column of men along the road from the station to the camp were somewhat lax, talking and laughing together and not paying close attention to their prisoners. The men marched along the right-hand side of the road; there were ditches at the edges, presumably to receive heavy rainfall that would otherwise flood the road. Max saw the possibility of letting himself disappear into a ditch, remaining there as the columns moved on. Quickly he rejected the idea. The country and village people were well aware that a stranger wandering in their midst was undoubtedly a camp escapee and would be fearful of offering him aid or protection. The location was at too great a distance from the border of Portugal or any place of refuge to make an escape feasible. Thus Max and the other prisoners arrived at Miranda after 3 days in boxcars and a long march from the train. Very soon after they reached Miranda they began to look back upon the bean-and-vegetable "feasts" at Caldas with longing, by comparison with their current conditions.

Max was confined to the Miranda de Ebro concentration camp for five months. The camp population numbered about four to five thousand prisoners. Barbed wire fences edged the limits of the camp and armed guards were stationed at the fences, one at an interval of 50 feet from the next guard. A prisoner attempting to come closer to a fence than within 10 feet was shot without question. Armed guards marched up and down all footpaths and walkways throughout the camp. Huge floodlights which made the camp as bright at night as in daylight led to prisoners' complaints that they inhibited sleep. These protests went unheeded under the strict security mandates in force.

The men slept in barracks, but no longer on the ground as had been the condition in Gerona. Bunk beds were provided, four decked beds to each bunk, with the topmost as the most desirable if one were an acrobat. In the stifling heat of the summer it afforded the best chance for a breath of air. Max secured a top berth for himself. Reveille wasn't really needed: a man's stomach pangs of hunger urged him to wakefulness at daybreak. Two prisoners of each barrack went to the kitchen with a huge container. They returned with the container filled with a hot liquid that simulated coffee. Each man was given a small loaf of bread. At noon another meal was provided. This consisted of a soup which varied in thickness and contents depending upon what cheap vegetables were obtainable for the camp. An orange completed the meal. Soup again for the evening meal. The soups were a lottery in which a lucky man was one whose bowl a bit of fat or suet was ladled into.

The camaraderie among the men that had existed in Gerona was considerably diminished in Miranda. Groupings according to nationality were decidedly evident. The men registered as British stopped sharing their 35 peseta weekly allowance with other prisoners. They kept to themselves their articles of clothing and the few other modest creature comforts issued only to British prisoners by the British Consul in Burgos and Madrid. These were not available to other nationals, even the Canadians who envied Max, a self-declared Palestinian receiving much better treatment. Max continued to abstain from smoking despite his intense desire for a cigarette. Instead he used his 80 cigarettes each week to barter for food which he could obtain from black-marketeering guards. Since the Civil War tobacco was rationed and this restriction remained in effect, giving rise to the high unofficial prices for black market purchases. Besides the superior treatment, the prisoners registered as British were the first to be released from Miranda, for it was Britain that concluded successful ransom negotiations with Spain before any other allied country.

Instructive courses given by qualified prisoners were a morale-boosting practice that began in Caldas and was permitted to continue in Miranda. Professors gave lectures in various subjects and held classes to teach English so that foreigners going to England upon their release would have a head-start on the language. Professional athletes led groups in calisthenics, body-building and competitive sports. These activities mitigated the loneliness, depression and anxiety often rampant in a prison situation of idleness and uncertainty. They also afforded vital distraction from the gnawing hunger of those long months. Everyone knew release would ultimately come if one followed the rules so as not to be shot. It was just a matter of trying to stay healthy. But when would the release come? When? When?

As they got deeper and deeper into the summer season the heat made the barracks stifling and unbearable with so many in a small area. The men were weakened by their diet of little protein and few calories and had little resistance to the exhausting heat. They grew dispirited by the tight security and the uncertainty surrounding their release. Cut off from their families they grew worried and anxious about wives, children and parents who were in war zones, or perhaps other camps. Each man felt himself alone in that huddled mass of wasting prisoners.

Max recalled that the men, said to be unfit for military service due to frailty, were all subject to inoculations against infectious diseases. When Max observed the rusted hypodermic needles as he stood in the long line of prisoners waiting to receive injections he gave a sign to one of the guards with whom he was on rather friendly terms. As the guard approached, Max furtively fingered the pack of cigarettes in his pocket. He whispered in Spanish, "No injection for me, please." *"No lo puedo,* Marco, I can't do that," the guard replied. He indicated a window at which the chief medical officer was standing and looking down upon the procedure below. The guard walked back to the table where he was part of the team doing the inoculations. But when Max's turn came the guardia shifted his position sufficiently so that the medical officer's view of what the guard was doing was obscured. He merely pretended to administer the inoculation, then shoved Max along and motioned the next man in line to step forward.

One day a committee of International Red Cross representatives was escorted through the camp on its tour of inspection. Early in the morning, before the arrival of the committee incredible changes began to take place. Sheets and blankets were brought to the barracks and the men were ordered to make up their beds. Then the prisoners were issued clean and presentable garments and told to put them on. A huge swimming pool in the courtyard, always dirty and dry was scoured and filled with sparkling water. From the cook house a medley of delicious aromas filled the camps dense air. The men were alert and hopeful. At noon two of the inspectors of the Red Cross came to talk to the men of Max's barracks. They asked pointed and precise questions about the conditions of the camp. The men replied that they were well treated, very adequately fed and clothed. There was nothing else to say, for the questioning was in the presence of camp officials. Only a fool would report the truth in view of the reprisals certain to follow an accurate description of circumstances.

As the interviews came to an end the camp chefs made an appearance, dressed in bright white uniforms, including starched chefs' hats rather than their usual dirty and sweat-stained T-shirts and trousers. They entered with rolling tables. These were wheeled in laden with meat, fresh vegetables, aromatic white bread, and mouth-watering fruit tarts. The men waited at attention expectantly and longingly. The committee departed. The lunch tables were hastily wheeled out, the wonderful food then to be served to the officers of the camp. Two guardias came to the barracks, ordered the men to strip their beds and to return the sheets and blankets that had been distributed from the supply closets of the hospital building. The swimming pool was drained and the water collected in barrels and tanks for use in the various parts of the camp. The traditional watery soup was the lunch fare that day, as every day.

The prisoners were not required to attend mass here at Miranda as had been the rule in Gerona. But at intervals chaplains from outside the camp made visits to the prisoners to give spiritual help to those who wished it. One day two priests arrived with cartons of Bibles. Who wanted one? Everyone reached out eagerly. The priests were noticeably touched by the response. They left, never knowing how much the men valued the silky paper of these sacred volumes as welcomed improvement over the rough newspaper available for personal hygiene in the latrines.

In late August 1942, the dozen British prisoners, Max among them were, given the order to prepare for release. They felt like bridegrooms on their wedding day as they dressed in a suit and a tie which had been issued each man by the consul. They strutted proudly, but with some embarrassment among the envious men who felt regret over their own uncertain fate but who did offer expressions of happiness for these being released. It was good-bye and good luck, hopes for those left behind, then off to the station, aboard a train, and on to Madrid, in the company of two Spanish officers.

Upon arrival the twelve released men were taken by their

official escorts to the British Embassy. It was here that Max requested the correction of his nationality on his records, admitting that he was not a British subject but in actuality a Frenchman. He stated it was his intention to serve with the Free French Battalions in England. *"Les Forces Francaises Libre"* were under the leadership of General Charles de Gaulle and attached to the Royal Air Force. There were French forces in North Africa as well, but Max requested attachment to a squadron in England.

The men were then taken to a hospital for comprehensive examinations, and following these a treatment plan for each man was formulated. For the next two months Max was still plagued by the dysentery he contracted during his imprisonment. Gradually his weakened body had to be nourished, his weight brought up from 90 pounds to his normal 155 pounds and eventually he was restored to strength and vigor.

Hundreds of released foreign prisoners were in Madrid, now housed in the best hotels of the city. Max and the eleven men released from Miranda with him were assigned individual rooms, each with its private bathroom at the Hotel del Medio Dia, on the Plaza Atocha. The elation they felt by such comfort and privacy was overwhelming and remained vivid to Max's senses. Nor could he ever forget what it meant to again have sufficient food. As for freedom, it was to him a continual miracle.

All the former prisoners had their meals in the hotel dining room. When heaped-up baskets of bread were brought to the table of "The Twelve," each roll looked to the men like a gold nugget. In a moment the baskets were empty. The waiter brought more, and these disappeared just as quickly. But the waiters were unperturbed and exchanged knowing smiles, for they were familiar with the reactions of other men recently out of the camps. Conditioned to hoard food, now they instinctively slipped the warm fresh rolls into their pockets and inside their shirts, squirreling them away for tomorrow when they would be hungry. The waiters knew that after a day or two their guests would feel secure enough, their fears would be overcome, and their hoarding instinct would dissipate. But until there was bread left on the table the waiters were instructed to continually replenish the supply, and to avert their gaze from the men's furtive gestures of hiding food.

The next day after coming to Madrid Max asked if he could have clothes that fit his emaciated body. He looked ludicrous, and his shoes were uncomfortably large. The Red Cross gave him a new wardrobe. The administrator there said they would keep the recently issued garments he had traveled in from Miranda so he could again wear them, probably in a few weeks when there would be an adequate weight gain to fill them out.

After a good breakfast each morning the men could circulate freely in the city. But there were many formalities to attend to. Treatments and examinations were scheduled at the hospital; at the Embassy there were forms and documents to be completed and signed. But otherwise they were unrestricted by the British authorities. The Spanish government required registration with the city police, as it does not only for all foreign visitors and foreign residents but for all Spaniards as well. An identification card was issued, stamped each week by the police. This card also included rations for cigarettes. Max did not resume smoking until he arrived in England, a habit he practiced to excess, for the next 18 years. While in Madrid he sold his ration of cigarettes on the flourishing black market.

Administrative formalities at the British Embassy took little time, but the men visited the building a good deal to have news of the war and to be in contact with compatriots.

Urns of hot chocolate, also snack foods and food supplements were always available there. The men were encouraged to take nourishment in between the scheduled hotel meals so that they would more rapidly return to health and normal weight. The war was impatiently anticipating and awaiting their active service; the sooner the better. Max and his buddies strolled the parks and boulevards of the city, and found distraction in the local movie houses.

In the evenings there were dances, cafes and cabarets. During these balmy summer evenings there was dancing in the park where young people gathered to meet each other and where older people nostalgically and wistfully watched the dancing and listened to the music. On one such evening Max met a young girl, 17 years old, accompanied by her mother. The two young people danced; they talked as best they could with Max's limited Spanish. After that they kept meeting by arrangement, always there in the park. Soon Carmelita began to appear unchaperoned. The girl, well bred, was of a traditional middle-class Spanish family. After agreeing to go to the movies and to places less visible to public scrutiny, Carmelita shyly but tactfully fended off Max's overtures to intimacy. She explained she was a virgin and that it was not permitted that she abandon her intact state before marriage. "All-the-way" was taboo; however her attraction to Max and her natural inclinations led to extensive caressing. They began to go to Max's room when the evenings grew late. There, Carmelita, who the young man called *"Mon Ange D'Espagne,"* My Spanish Angel, remained at the hotel with him until the stroke of 11:30, returning home before her family's curfew could be violated. In motherly fashion Carmelita saw "Marco" to his bed and kissed him tenderly before hurrying out into the night.

The young girl's passion and emotion proved stronger than her religion or the traditions of the petite bourgeoisie.

One night she intimated her acquiescence but Max's honor—or maybe prudence—mandated their continued restrained behavior. He told Carmelita it would be a very unwise act which would inevitably only cause her pain afterward because he had a wife in France and very soon he must leave Spain to fight in the war. After that, if he survived he must return to his own country.

Max's stay in Madrid lasted six weeks. When he moved on to Gibraltar he felt strong and fit, although his intestinal disorder was not yet completely cured. Max paid a visit to the home of Carmelita's family prior to leaving Madrid. Before the completion of the formal good-byes to the girl and her family, Carmelita's brother closeted himself with Max and inquired as to the nature of the relationship that had existed between the Frenchman and the young Spanish maiden. Max speaking candidly, in broken Spanish put the man at ease when he assured him that the purity of his sister remained unviolated. Now he knew for certain that he had acted wisely. An aching heart can be healed, but for the girl who gave herself before marriage there was little to look forward to. Upper and middle class young women of Spain had no future outside of becoming a wife and mother and a good marriage was available only to a young virgin.

A trainload of men set off for La Linea. From that point they crossed a bridge on foot and then were on the British soil of Gibraltar. At the bridge there was a formal exchange as the Spanish authorities handed the men over to the British authorities. Civilians watched and waved. Good-bye, *Adios*. Go With God, *Vaya Con Dios*. Good Luck, *Buena Suerta*.

Chapter Eight
Though I Die, I Dare

The stopover in Gibraltar lasted several days. Through the French Embassy in Madrid Max's military history had been verified; now, in Gibraltar the information was compiled into a new military book and issued to him. It was confirmed on his records that he had made a successful escape from the enemy and was fit for combat service with the Free French. In Gibraltar he also received several thousand British pounds, representing his accumulated military pay from the time he joined the Resistance, through the period of transit from France to Spain and the months in prisons and camps, followed by the weeks in Madrid.

The men were issued the colonial British uniform: short pants and safari jackets used in warm climates. All of them circulated around Gibraltar many using their time and money to make purchases. The island was filled with unrestricted goods that could be useful in England as saleable or tradeable. Max bought quantities of cigarettes and also silk articles, such as scarves. Soon the Frenchmen were separated from other nationals and ordered aboard a cruiser of the Free French. They proceeded to Setubal, Portugal to pick up other escapees, mostly high ranking officers who had succeeded in reaching Portugal without capture, or who had been liberated from Spain's detention centers and were waiting there to be transported to England.

The cruiser backtracked and went to Casablanca for a period of several days. The former prisoners and escapees of France were again mingled with those of other Allied nations where all of them were taken to guarded army barracks for individual security checks and de-briefing. After security clearance they received a uniform of American suntans, the summer uniform of the U.S. army. Passes were issued for free circulation in Casablanca.

The men had their first chance to see the new American military equipment such as the Jeep. They were encouraged to inspect and try out these latest war "toys." Perhaps a motive was to persuade the undecided to officially sign up for active duty. This was the ultimate moment of decision, the last chance to decline to serve. No pressure was exerted but most men elected to enlist. For Max there had never been a moment of hesitation or doubt. He had gone underground and later fled Nazi occupation so as not to risk going as a lamb to slaughter. Now he would fight from a defensible position: with weaponry, in an arena of equality.

Next, the men were transported to Algiers on a convoy train of Allied troops; from the train they boarded the British troop ship, *The Samaria*. The ship was densely surrounded by escort vessels and protected overhead by fighter planes. It bobbed, weaved and circled, taking several weeks, sailing almost to the coast of North America before reaching Liverpool, England.

*   *   *

September in Liverpool was fiercely cold, with sharp, biting winds. The summer uniforms had to be hastily replaced by winter woolens before the men left the ship. Of the perhaps 10,000 men aboard those who had come from Spain were moved under heavy guard to London where they were confined to a camp until security clearance allowed their release. Fears of enemy infiltrators, slipping in among them, required these procedures.

Six weeks of pre-combat training took place at an air base in Preswick, Scotland. Thirty miles from Glasglow, the men

138

alternately rehearsed in these war games as both teams of combatants—Allied and Axis—air corpsmen. Allied planes were painted and decorated with the insignia of the German Messerschmitt, to be recognized, stalked, attacked, and shot down in this prelude to the combat missions soon to follow.

Mechanics taught the basics of recognizing the source of technical problems, dismantling non-functioning parts, then replacing them quickly and expertly as possible in order to carry on.

Physical fitness involving vigorous calisthenics and competitive games were of particular importance for Max who, grooming to be a rear gunner, could not be allowed to become portly and no longer able to slip into the narrow passage to the gun turret. Training in simulators was employed to condition the airmen against air sickness.

Recreation was confined to the base area. It frequently included films, taken during veritable action. The female military personnel were a source of dance partners, and to share some drinks, social games, and conversation. Lack of privacy, besides strict regulation precluded "in-depth" relationships, except clandestinely, which was risky.

Lessons in elementary first aid were taught by the medical corps and every man paid careful attention to the means by which he might be able to save his own life or that of another man in the crew. A kit containing essentials that included morphine was issued, to be placed in a patch pocket in the mid calf of the left trouser leg.

All instruction for the French-speaking corpsmen was given first in English, then repeated in French. The manuals and homework were read and written in whichever language a man was most familiar with. Exams were rigid, as were the physical and psychological screenings; about 12 to 15% of training recruits washed out before completion. "Graduation" was rewarded with a 3-day pass, and the commencement of combat flight pay. A final message was the emphatic warning of the risk of contracting a venereal disease during the 3 days that most graduates would spend in London. A packet of condoms and after-the-fact hygienic liquid was handed out to the eager young lions.

Max headed directly for the Scottish Jewish community service club as the source of his female companionship and socializing. Native Jewish young men were absent in the war and foreigners of the same religious faith were well sought after. This scarcity, and the normal popularity enjoyed by French-Jewish airmen among the "Jewish Princesses" and families gave Max unlimited opportunities for diversion whenever he had a pass to leave the base.

Entree was immediate for Max, for it was aboard *The Samaria* that he had met a Jewish-Scottish soldier, wounded in the Middle-East encounter, who suggested that Max contact his parents when he was in Scotland. They were more than happy to introduce him to friends who quickly extended dinner invitations, particularly those families that had unmarried daughters.

Max relates:

"The focus of my life until the defeat of the enemy—acknowledged to be a formidable foe—was my job as a tail gunner in the Halifax heavy bomber. It earned the macabre nickname 'The Flying Coffin.' I hoped for survival but knew how remote were my chances; casualties were running close to 80% for the gunners. During training in the simulators, I became well aware of the exposed position of the tail gunner, and with the fact that the machine gun I would be operating was limited in its course to 180 degrees. The speed and mobility of the German fighter planes enabled them to aim for the gunner's unprotected back if the bombers pilots were not made aware of the approaching fighter plane, or if he could not maneuver the slow, very cumbersome bomber quickly enough to avoid successful attack."

When the bombers set out from their base in Britain,

they were well escorted by their Royal Air Force fighter planes. However, the missions over Germany were too far for the fighter planes to fly on the limited fuel they were able to carry. At a certain point the fighters turned back, and the bombers were on their own. Without their own fighters to fend off the attacks of both enemy bombers and fighters, they were extremely vulnerable.

In 1943, when Max began the first of the 29 missions in which he participated as a rear gunner, a member of the Free French, attached to the Royal Air Force, he was 31 years old. That was considered too old for the assignment, but at his insistence it was given to him. He was good-naturedly dubbed "pops" by the 18 to 20 year olds that were the usual ages of members of the crews.

Apart from his age, for Max there was another issue that was brought up to him before his missions over Germany.

"As a Jew, Neuman, we have every reason to believe that if you are shot down or have to bail out in German territory, it is not likely that the rules of war as defined and established by the Geneva Convention will protect you from the Nazis. It is my duty to advise you that we excuse you from taking part in these missions."

"Thank you sir. I volunteered for the purpose of fighting the *Boche*. These are the missions I most want to be engaged in," was Max's impassioned reply.

Before each mission, every man was given a portfolio in which to put a letter or letters to loved ones, and small mementos to be given to his loved ones should he not survive the mission. The portfolio was sealed. Its contents were returned at the end of the mission if one came back alive. A briefing was convened before the mission; a debriefing followed the return to the base. Each man gave his report. The reports were synthesized, conclusions drawn, plans for the next mission were formulated. Weather reports and forecasts were crucial to the timing of missions, but so was the information gleaned from completed missions.

When a pass was issued to leave the base—on occasions without official leave, as well—Max spent the time in London, the venue of frenetic diversion for servicemen and civilians, all desperate to put aside momentarily the misery of war torn Britain: the deprivations, rationing of even the most basic consumer products, the loss of family members, friends, and neighbors. Some living in London at the time were there temporarily, displaced by wartime employment or military service. Children were scarcely seen, having been sent to the countryside for reasons of their safety, some even to far-off Canada. And of course, there was perpetual sorrow over the growing numbers of deaths among the service men and women, as well as the civilians killed during the bombing raids that were relentless and unremitting.

There was an intensity, an urgent impulse to dispel or ignore the fear and heightened anxiety that at any moment enemy bombs might rain down, showering their destructive effects, annihilating people and buildings. It was demoralizing and devastating to lose a home, along with the bits and pieces of personal property to which one attaches great emotion. Those reminders of special life cycle events: weddings, christenings, birthdays, school graduations, tender memories kept alive by numerous tangible objects. How overwhelming was the sorrow to lose a photo album, a marriage certificate, the family Bible, grandmother's delicate tea cups. These, suddenly and wantonly lost, shattered the stability and continuity of life. Mode and mood of normal living were utterly changed.

Don't think! Don't feel! Seize, grasp any fragile straw extended in this moment of time. Now, before it vanishes. The sounds of music? Dance, sing. Tasty food? Consume it, eat, drink without thought of moderation or prudence. Take the love of one who offers it, for it may well be the last caress in a young life that may never see old age. All was tentative. Tomorrow? Perhaps, but perhaps not. The din of loud music, loud voices in the pubs and servicemen's centers were frequently overpowered by the sudden, insistent wail of the sirens that announced a warning of an impending raid by enemy planes sited in the distance.

Max gives this description:

"Many hurried off the streets, or dismounted buses and trolleys that came to an abrupt halt. Some people headed for the nearest underground shelter. But many others resolutely continued whatever they were doing. They were very brave, disciplined, and remarkably self-controlled people. During the worst days of the 'blitz,' the British people continued to believe in their ultimate triumph, in their ability to survive the might of 'the Gerries.' The V-1 bombs whistled eerily as they descended; later there were the V-2's, hauntingly silent, which made them even more unnerving."

*   *   *

The allied bombing raids gradually destroyed the German factories and mines, weakened the military, undermined civilian morale, and the tide of war began to turn. After the D-Day June 6th landing on Normandy, and the liberation of France, Max was among the first to obtain a "leave of compassion" to go home for a short visit. He noted how thin and drawn his wife looked. Partly it was from the extremely limited food rations received by the French. The conquerors exercised their power to take most of what was produced. But also Ginette was feeling the strain of the serious illness of her young son who was in the hospital with osteomyelitis. The distraught mother was spending her days at the bedside of her little boy, helping to care for him during this time of great shortages of medical personnel.

The younger child, three-year-old Christianne, was in a boarding situation in the country. Max went to the hospital, stayed briefly, talking encouragingly to Daniel, who had only a vague remembrance of his father. Then Ginette and Max, both overwhelmed by the flood of feelings that took hold of them, hurried out of the hospital to a nearby cafe for their first meal together: their first moments to exchange private, personal sentiments reflected the aching void of the past two-and-a-half years that Max had been absent. Their first renewal of intimacy came after the lunch and the taxi ride back to their apartment. Their love-making was unhurried, intense; it blunted—for its duration, and for the next few hours—the hideous memories of those years that encompassed the start of the war, the fall of France, the occupation by the Germans, which took their toll on every one in France. Anger, bitterness, frustration, and grief were pervasive among the French people. Traditionally frugal, the insecurities justified turning them grasping, greedy, quarrelsome, and self-absorbed.

The day that followed this first day in Paris, at the apartment, which Max had not seen during the four years of his service to the Resistance in the south of France and the subsequent years in Spain and England, he enjoyed a leisurely breakfast and reading the newspapers. At noon, Ginette went to the hospital and Max took the train for an hour's visit with his little daughter whom he had not seen since she was seven months old.

As Max approached the farmhouse, a middle-aged woman opened the creaking screen door and came out to greet him. He was expected, for Ginette had telephoned her that morning. The woman wiped her hands with her apron, brushed away wisps of graying hair that had escaped the ribbon that was holding the rest of her hair to the back of her florid neck. *"Bienvenue,"* she said, smilingly, then called over her shoulder: "Christianne, Christianne, *voici ton papa."* Here is your daddy. A small, delicate-looking three-year-old girl, dressed in a flowered pinafore and little brown sandals emerged from the house. She looked uncertainly at the man. Her wide hazel eyes expressed a mixture of shyness and curiosity. Then the child took one step forward, extended a thin little hand as she spoke timidly: "Bon jour, monsieur." Good day, sir. This was the feeble start of a father-daughter relationship which would never achieve the hearty blossoming of harmony and deep commitment. Max longed for it all the rest of his life, did not have the ability to achieve it, and died regretting his loss.

Max returned to the base in England when his leave came to an end. Soon, the war in Europe concluded, then the war in the Pacific came to an end. The world turned attention to the mending, healing, rebuilding, and the effort to put the war behind. It was a time to look forward, not backward. That was what Max Neuman determined to do. He was fortunate enough to have forty-eight more years of life. It was his misfortune to remain in the savage grip of trauma up to the very last few days, when he finally appeared to cast off the shackles that bound his psyche, when at last he surrendered, but only to the peaceful drift that propelled him from this world to—what?—the unknown.

Post Script

I have written of a time that I did not know in the way my husband did, of places I have never seen—or am barely acquainted with—and of people whose experiences were so different from my own that I feel I am only *technically* the author of this work. Strictly speaking, I am a conduit through which my husband transmitted the story, in all its detail, to you the reader. It is as he remembered this period of his life, and related it to me. If deviations in facts exist: names, events, they are unintentional and can only be explained by errors in memory.

Of lesser knowledge, but contained in my manuscript is Helena Rubenstein as part of a close-knit family, many members holding key positions in her business. Woven into my story are vignettes of Mme. Rubinstein, her sister and brother-in-law, the Hirschbergs, nephew Oscar Kolin, Edgar Titus, publisher who was Helena's first husband, and the father of her two sons, Roy and Horace.

The Rubinstein anecdotes are depicted because Helen was a first cousin to Max's mother, and for many years their lives were entwined.

The fame and mystique of Helen Rubinstein is worldwide for her development of beauty preparations and cosmetics. From the humble beginning as s young Russian Jewish immigrant to Australia, she built an international company and a great fortune. Her career in skin care products started in Australia in response to the dry climate of that great continent, which caused early wrinkling and aging of women's skin, as well as unsightly redness from exposure to the merciless sunshine by a population that spent much time outdoors.

Assured of the positive acceptance of the formulae she had developed, the perfumes and packaging that enhanced the appeal of the face and body creams, and the lines of powders and rouges, the budding female executive expanded her enterprise to Paris, France—the world's capital of high fashion for women.

As she grew more wealthy, Helena Rubinstein's aura also embraced her great philanthropies, particularly in the arts. Even today, her elder son, Roy Titus, maintains her ongoing contributions to leading museums, including the National Holocaust Museum in Washington, D.C.

*   *   *

The city of Lizensk, Poland, gained world-wide fame as a spiritual center for a form of Judaism known as Hasidism. Rabbi Elimelech settled there and spread this mystical emphasis on Jewish thought and practice. He died 21 Adar, 1786. Thousands of Jews travel to Lizensk on that date as a pilgrimage to do honor to this revered rabbi.

Generations of Max's family have been faithful adherents to Hasidic Judaism. The book, *The Kabbalah and Jewish Mysticism* by Israel Gutwirth, Part II, pages 165-168 are the source for the details of Rabbi Elimelech and his doctrin.